The Celibacy Myth

Charles A. Gallagher
Thomas L. Vandenberg

THE
CELIBACY
MYTH

Loving for Life

 St Paul Publications

St Paul Publications
Middlegreen, Slough SL3 6BT, England

Copyright © 1987 by Charles A. Gallagher and
Thomas L. Vandenberg

First published in 1988 by The Crossroad Publishing Company,
370 Lexington Avenue, New York, N.Y. 10017, USA

Printed in USA

ISBN 085439 295 5

St Paul Publications is an activity of the priests and brothers of
the Society of St Paul who proclaim the Gospel through the media
of social communication

To the Catholic Priests
of the United States

Contents

Acknowledgments

While this book is the combined effort of two priests living on separate coasts of our country, its inspiration comes from countless priests and married couples who live everywhere in between. Special thanks go to Pete and Nancy Wright who helped create a workshop on celibacy from a couple's point of view, and to Worldwide Marriage Encounter for sponsoring this workshop at its 1983 national conventions in San Francisco, St. Louis, and Philadelphia. Thanks also to Bob and Ethel Reber and Father Mike Walsh, O.F.M. who helped us grasp the significance of celibate masculinity. Appreciated as well are the observations of several participants of the master's program in Christian community development at Regis College in Denver, Colorado. Finally, thanks to those countless priests who know the joys and sorrows of living close to their people.

Introduction

There are two predictable reactions to the title of this book, *The Celibacy Myth*. The first says something like, "It's about time someone blew the whistle on this celibacy hoax." The second says, "I wish those troublemakers would leave celibacy alone." Ironically, both of these reactions reflect an incomplete understanding of "myth." This is to be expected, since most people popularly regard a myth as a fictitious story. When we grew up, myth was in the same category as an "old wives' tale," often a story about the gods of ancient times. It had existence only in the world of imagination. Therefore, from this vantage point, to speak of celibacy as a myth is to imply that there is something fanciful, unreal, and possibly even deceptive about it. To some, this is a welcomed admission; to others, it is an unwelcomed attack.

However, there is another way of looking at the concept of "myth." Rather than seeing it only as something fanciful, myth also has a very different, even contrasting, meaning. It speaks to something real that is deep inside us as human beings, like the most profound longings of the human heart. From the myths that are a part of us arise our dreams about life. Scholars, like the psychologist Carl G. Jung, regard myth as something akin to a "collective unconscious" common to all people. Myths seem to provide us with an intuitive vision of reality that helps us interpret what it means. They somehow seem to spring from human nature itself. In very nontechnical language, our myths have something to do with our "gut feelings" about life, common to all people. Rather than arising from our imagination, myths in this sense give rise to our imagination and grope for concrete expression in life.

This is less than an adequate description of myth, but it is in this sense that we are using it here. Many scholars have developed this notion in great detail for those who wish to pursue it further. The point in mentioning it at all is an attempt to help us think about celibacy at a level that goes below the surface of what we read and hear most of the time. The myths of human life are not to be taken lightly. Furthermore, since God is the creator of all, we might look at the way God predisposed or "programed" us to be the source of our myths. Could this be why the life of Jesus, his message, and his Gospel have such universal appeal? He is the fullest expression of what it means to be human. Free of distortion, his vision of life is one that excites and captivates since it speaks to the deepest longings of the human heart, to the common myths that enliven us.

It is within this context that we will be looking at the issue of celibacy. What is the underlying myth behind this practice in the church? What longings of the human heart does it speak to? What does it have to do with the Gospel that Jesus preached? What is its place in the church? In short, why celibacy?

In many ways, *The Celibacy Myth* is ultimately about the church. While celibacy can be spoken of in a secular context, such a focus would miss its most revealing insights necessary for our reflection. Celibacy has to do with people and how these people relate to one another. But what these people bring to their relationship, how they view life and its ultimate meaning, will profoundly shape their attitude about the significance of the relationships they have. Therefore, for our considerations here, it is critical that we bring a faith-dimension to our discussion of celibacy, since faith speaks directly to how we view life. While it is not necessary that the reader be Roman Catholic, it is helpful that he/she appreciates the Roman Catholic faith reflected in this book. The understanding of celibacy we are presenting here requires people whose belief in the church is integral to their Christian faith. Their faith must embrace the church, not because the church is needed to provide fellowship, but because the people believe they are called to a unity with one another as the Body of Christ that will give their proclamation of the Gospel credibility to the world. Celibacy can best be understood in this context. In one way or the other, celibacy is meant ultimately to assist the church in its proclamation of the Gospel and thereby to further the Kingdom of God in our world.

It is neither the purpose nor is it within the scope of this book to debate the relative merits of a celibate priesthood. This is not to say this issue is unworthy of serious reflection and discussion in the church. Rather, our purpose is to concentrate on the meaning of celibacy itself as a charism in, of, and for the church. It is hoped, however, that what is said here will contribute in some positive way to the thinking of those who discuss the value of celibacy for the church. Their discussion must embrace three aspects of the issue: what is best for the priest himself, the faithful, and the proclamation of the Gospel. To focus attention only on one of these factors of the "celibate equation" would be an injustice to the other two.

Should celibacy ever become optional in the Latin Rite of the Catholic Church, the options have to be clear to those who are being asked to make that choice. That choice, by the way, is not just the priest's to make, for it is also a choice that must be made by the faithful. As a charism of relationship, celibacy requires that both parties to that relationship are willing to assume responsibility for it. This means that the other party, the faithful, needs to be educated about the nature of celibacy as well as prospective candidates for the priesthood, not to mention those already ordained. What is said in these pages, therefore, is directed toward the laity, religious, and clergy alike.

Unfortunately, the word "celibacy" does not enjoy a very good image with many people. It is seen simply as a law that forbids someone to marry or have sexual involvement with another. This popular notion carries with it the underlying implication that there must be something inferior about marriage and immoral about sex. This has certainly been evident in much of the media's discussion surrounding the issue of celibacy. It is as though the church were still imposing celibacy on her priests to protect them from something below their dignity as priests. Sadly, this notion may even be held by some Catholics. The discouraging consequence is that many have not only developed very narrow and negative views of celibacy, but they have also been led to view marriage as a second-class vocation in the church, unworthy of one who celebrates the sacred mysteries for the church. Given the existence of such misguided thinking, it is hardly a wonder that the issue of celibacy is so fraught with emotion and unyielding opinions. When celibacy appears as a vestige of another age, it cannot help but be regarded as having been mistakenly passed over during the updating that took place with the Second Vatican Council.

Ironically, it is the sacrament of matrimony, currently undergoing its own awakening as an instrument of renewal in the church, that is beginning to shed light on the meaning of celibacy in the church. As a sign of Christ's love for the church, the sacramental couple have much to say to their brothers and sisters in faith about relationship. Just as the couple relationship is unique among human relationships, the relationship that exists among the members of the Body of Christ should be unique among human relationships. While there are many communities that exist in the human family, there is none that is called to such intimacy and communion as is the community of the church. Celibacy, as we shall try to show, can exist with a positive influence only to the degree that this communion exists or is being positively pursued by the people of the church. When the church is issue-oriented, at the expense of relationship, then the value of celibacy is bound to become lost in a shroud of mystery. To most, it will be reduced to just another issue needing attention. The further we drift from a sense of community with one another in the church, the harder it will be to comprehend any saving value to a law that calls for a celibate clergy.

Contrary to common opinion, a celibate is not supposed to live in isolation from his people. That would be as pointless as expecting a husband to live in isolation from his wife. The point of celibacy is not to show people how to live alone but to facilitate their living together. Celibacy is not an excuse to hang a "Do-Not-Disturb" sign in front of the parish house. To the contrary, it is a gift of the Spirit that invites a priest to be accessible to his people. While he is bound to benefit personally, celibacy is ultimately for the sake of his people and for the building up of the church as a community of faith. Of its nature, celibacy is not meant to be lived in private. It is a call to relationship.

Since the sacramental couple can speak of the value of relationship to the church in a most powerful and effective way, and since celibacy is a charism of relationship for the church, the basic thesis of this book, the matrimonied couple is in a unique position to speak to the issue of celibacy. There is no conflict between celibacy and marriage. In fact, they are mutually supportive of each other. Just as celibate priests are in an advantageous position to call married couples to a sacramental way of life for the church, matrimonied couples are in a similar position to assist the priest in his commitment to a celibate way of life for the church.

It is necessary that we approach this issue of celibacy with an adult faith. While a child's faith does not make distinctions between what is central to being a Christian and what is not central, an adult faith is able to acknowledge a hierarchy of beliefs that we hold as followers of Christ. For instance, the teaching of the resurrection of Jesus is so important, so emphatically present in scripture and tradition, that Christians literally build their lives around it. If this were somehow proven to be untrue, the faith of the people would be utterly destroyed. They would have to leave the church. In fact, the church as they had understood it would simply cease to exist. It would, more accurately, "leave" them. On the other hand, some truths of our faith are not so critical. For example, the dogma of the Assumption, a truth of our Catholic faith that was not defined until 1950 by Pope Pius XII, would be in this category. In saying this, we are in no way implying that this teaching is optional to Catholics, nor that it is less true than other teachings of the church. For centuries, however, the believing faithful had not even heard of this teaching as such, so it could not be considered central to our faith as Catholics. Consequently, if it were somehow proven to be untrue, our faith would not be destroyed.

This does not mean that the Immaculate Conception is not an important teaching in the Catholic Church. It says only that it is not central. The church can exist without it. What is so important about this "peripheral" teaching is that it does say something very significant about a central teaching of our faith, without which our faith would crumble: Jesus is Savior of all people. In effect, what the Immaculate Conception proclaims is that the power of Jesus as Savior is so monumental that it saved Mary from the first moment of her conception. While we as Catholics are not intended to build our lives around Mary as such, we are meant to build our lives around all she stands for in relation to Jesus. In honoring Mary, we ultimately "rejoice in God my savior" with her (Luke 1:47). Her Immaculate Conception directs us to Jesus as Savior of all.

Celibacy is not central to our Catholic faith either. This comes as no surprise, although there may be those Catholics who have such strong feelings about this issue that if the Church were to change its legislation and allow a married clergy, they might consider leaving the Catholic Church. On the other hand, some have already left the Church over this issue, especially as it has affected their personal lives. As we have said before, the question of optional celibacy deserves to be addressed.

If celibacy, however, is to be seen as more than simply a discipline of the church, it must, as a "peripheral" teaching, say something important about some central doctrine of the church to justify any place of universal respectability it may hope to enjoy. Let us suggest that that doctrine is the church itself, not so much as institution, but as the Body of Christ. In the teaching of Jesus, there is nothing "peripheral" about the church being a united people of faith. "May they all be one. Father, may they be one in us, as you are in me and I am in you" (John 17:21). St. Luke speaks of the church as a "community of believers" (Acts 4:32). St. Paul develops the significance of this community as the "Body of Christ" (I Cor. 12). The Second Vatican Council introduced the phrase "the People of God" (*Dogmatic Constitution on the Church*, chapter 2). This is why celibacy has value in the church. It is a special gift, a charism offered to some in the church to facilitate the sense of communion and intimacy that all the members of the church are to have with one another. Unity is an essential mark of the church. To give up on this is to give up on the church. And to give up on the church, for a Catholic, is to give up on being a follower of

Jesus. Like Jesus, the way the members of the church live with one another should proclaim a way of life that touches something deep inside those outside the church—the myth that underlies the deepest longings of their hearts. In other words celibacy, optional or otherwise, has little value in itself. But when it is seen in its relationship to the church as the Body of Christ, it directs us to a truth of our faith that is not optional at all: our unity with one another in Christ.

It must be said that the only atmosphere in which this charism of the Spirit can grow is the one created by the faith in which the celibate lives. Unless he is breathing the air of faith through his commitment to Jesus Christ by a life of dedicated prayer, he can neither enter nor live a celibate way of life. The issue is not so much his allowing God to enter his life, as it is to see his time of prayerful reflection, contemplation, and meditation as his entering more fully into God's life. God alone is the reality that can give purpose and meaning to a celibate priest's life. Without a life of communion with Jesus, he is bound to lose his way. His view of self and vision for the church depend on it. In other words, rather than seeing celibacy as a call to be alone with God, we see spending time alone with God to be absolutely necessary for a priest to live the kind of celibate relationship he is expected to live with his people. When a celibate priest hears Jesus say, "Apart from me you can do nothing" (John 15:5), he knows those words were meant especially for him.

Finally, celibacy is a charism that is not limited to those ordained to the presbyterate, as it is one of the major vows required for membership in most religious communities. Religious brothers and sisters, as well as priests, are called to live a celibate way of life within their respective religious communities for the sake of the church. Even some lay people have chosen to live a life of celibacy as part of their commitment to the church. The focus of this book, however, is limited to celibacy as a charism to be lived by priests in relationship to their people. It is hoped that the principles that apply in this case will apply or be adaptable to other celibates in the church. In any case, it can be a source of reflection and study for all the faithful in the church who are entrusted with proclaiming the Gospel of Jesus Christ with the greatest possible credibility, "so the world may believe" (John 17:21).

1

Privation or Privilege?

Whenever the subject of celibacy comes up in a conversation, it is only a matter of moments until the question is asked, "Do you think celibacy should be compulsory for priests?" Considering the kind of publicity that surrounds this issue in the secular media, not to mention the Catholic press itself, this should come as no revelation to anyone. Even grade-school children are ready with questions about their priests' life style. Apparently celibacy has found its way into family discussions around the dinner table. Rather than being interested in why a man becomes a priest, more people seem intrigued by why he cannot be married.

That leads to another good question. What is it about a celibate priest that justifies his not marrying? Even if celibacy were optional, there must be some rather strong reasons why a priest would choose to live a celibate life style. It goes without saying that a negative view of marriage cannot be one of them. Were he to look upon the sacrament of matrimony as somehow beneath his dignity as a priest, or if he thought he was not capable of the responsibilities of marriage or afraid of intimacy, he would have no business being a priest. Before attempting an answer, however, it may be helpful to get in touch with one's own understanding of celibacy first. Drawing on personal experience, not on what one may have read already or can recall from seminary days, write down on a piece of paper a definition of celibacy.

What does celibacy mean? What is it all about? (Take a couple of minutes.)

What Is It?

If the reader is like most people, his or her tendency will be to write down what celibacy is not. Perhaps the response will be something like, "Celibacy is a law that forbids a priest to marry." While this is a true statement, it is not a definition of celibacy. Invariably this issue sets up celibacy and marriage as though they were opposites. This is a curious twist, for when someone asks what the opposite of a married man is, the answer never comes back "a celibate" but "a bachelor." The opposite of a married woman is not a nun but a spinster. Therefore, why do we think the opposite of a celibate man or celibate woman is a husband or wife? While celibacy and marriage are mutually exclusive, they need not be opposites. Nevertheless, this answer is enough to make us view celibacy negatively, as something unattractive, a privation. How can parents with this concept of celibacy be enthusiastic about their child's embracing it as a way of life? Such a notion of celibacy hardly justifies let alone defines it.

Perhaps the reader said something like, "Celibacy forbids sexual intimacy with another." This too is true, but it is not a definition of celibacy either. If anything, it describes a consequence of chastity. The nature of sexual intimacy excludes the celibate. But chastity is not the private domain of celibates, as it is part of every baptized person's call as a follower of Christ. Even married men and women are bound by a form of chastity in the context of their marriages. Celibacy is not, therefore, to be identified solely with the absence of genital activity. This mistaken notion serves only to cast another negative shadow over the meaning of celibacy. It shrouds any positive value it may have for the church. Yet this misconception, like the first, has taken its toll in the thinking of many good and sincere people.

An Example

Recently, a priest shared with me his rationale for leaving the priesthood to marry. Throughout our discussion, he identified celibacy with the law not to marry. He viewed it as an imposition, a form of oppression, an injustice against his basic human emotional need for intimate love. Celibacy was portrayed as a sentence imposed on him when he was ordained, and now his living a full life demanded he be free of it. He said he did not want to go the way he had seen so many other priests go before him, reverting to "cynicism, arbitrary authoritarianism, clinical aloofness, or various forms of escapism including dependency on alcohol and drugs." Celibacy was the culprit. Marriage, in his case, was the only alternative.

His fears were not without legitimacy, however, as we reflected on our seminary days and how celibacy was never adequately explained except in terms of not marrying. In those days, we were even advised to keep a certain "safe" distance from people, men as well as women. Somehow, by way of implication, this had something to do with the meaning of celibacy and a celibate life style.

The accuracy of these observations is not the issue here. At issue is the fact that our conversation to this point was not about celibacy at all. It was about an implication of celibacy, perhaps, but not celibacy. If celibacy is a charism of the church for the sake of the church, it cannot be something that is so void of any socially redeeming value. A charism is a God-given gift that is offered to someone for the building up of the church or for proclaiming the Gospel in some way. Rather than a privation, any real charism is a privilege.

A Matter of Perspective

As long as we continue to look at celibacy in terms of what a celibate "gives up," the positive side of this charism will never be addressed, let alone appreciated. For example, it would be foolish to look upon someone's choice to go on a diet only in terms of the chocolate sundaes that are sacrificed. Even a diabetic who chooses to stop eating sugar can take the sting out of it by seeing his choice as one that will foster a fuller life. Perhaps a better example is when someone gets married. John can focus his attention on either Teresa, his bride, the one he has chosen to spend his life with, or on Betty and Sue, two friends he used to date. Implicitly, he chose to renounce them. But it would be ridiculous to think he was preoccupied with them as Teresa walked down the aisle on their wedding day. He was not concerned with what he had "given up." He is too filled with his bride, and everyone at the wedding knows it.

For the sake of elaboration, however, let us say that John did focus on the renunciation aspect of his decision to marry Teresa. (There is truth to this dimension of his choice.) Rather than viewing his marriage as a going toward his wife, he would be looking upon it as a turning away from someone else. Rather than a positive act of entering into a relationship, he would see it as a negative act of giving up a relationship. Unfortunately, when he views his choice in this way, he is setting the stage for self-pity, iron-willed virtue, or infidelity and failure. His wife is bound to suffer drastically regardless of the path he chooses. The problem is not his marriage but how he is looking at it. Therefore, it is critical that John always remember he chose Teresa because he loves her, he wants her, he desires to immerse his life in her life and find his happiness in making her happy. He must remember the willingness he had to place himself in her hands — to say, "I trust you; I believe in you; I make myself yours."

A Charism of Relationship

This is the point of the celibacy charism. It is not a renunciation; it is an affirmation. Celibacy is a charism of relationship. It has to do with the relationship of a priest with his people, his bonding with them. It is about his placing his happiness in their hands, his act of faith that they will make his life fulfilling by the love they pour out on him. Celibacy is what enables a priest to say to the faithful, "I trust you; I believe you; I make myself yours." While it is not essential to priesthood, it is a unique grace that can enhance one's life as a priest. And while it would not be necessary to expect that all those who would like to be priests would be offered this charism, there is no question that all priests, celibate or married, are called to have a special relationship with the people for whom they were ordained.

The Nature of Priesthood

The way we view priests becomes critical here. Are they just ministers among many ministers in the church? Or is priesthood more than a ministry? It seems that so much of what is said about priesthood today is in terms of competence, accomplishments, and results. Priests are evaluated in terms of their performance of duties and activities. A priest's whole life is perceived as oriented toward doing good deeds and satisfying his people. What he does for them has become more important than who he is with them. While his activities may all be good and even commendable, is this primarily what priesthood is about, doing good deeds and meeting people's needs? There is no question that ministry like this has to happen in the church, but is not ministry really a charism of confirmation rather than of orders?

In many ways, priests can blur the meaning of confirmation for their people. As long as priests see themselves solely as the chief ministers in their parishes, they are going to hold their people back from the full expression of their sacramentality. To confuse the issue even more, many priests are beginning to see their "priestly activities" in terms of jobs to be performed for their people. This, in turn, is opening the door to the growing practice of living away from the people they are committed to serve. Their coming to the parish office each day is equivalent to their "going to work." The distinction between the clergy and laity becomes more fuzzy and difficult to distinguish in practice. And the more this happens, the more difficult it is to grasp any value in living alone as a celibate.

Attempts to justify celibacy in these circumstances center on seeing it as a technique or tactic to free the priest to have more time to give to his people. Celibacy is regarded as an asset for efficiency in performing priestly duties. It claims to free the priest to do more things and to attend more meetings. (No wonder it is suspect!) As most priests know, however, they would be hard pressed to prove married Protestant ministers do not spend as much time with their people and go to as many meetings as they do. Married clergy seem to be just as efficient as nonmarried priests.

What all this is saying is that if priesthood is primarily ministry, then celibacy is not intimately connected with priesthood. There is absolutely no real necessity for someone who is primarily involved in service to be celibate. He does not need to have a unique and intimate relationship to the people he serves. He just has to be good at it. Of course, he has to be nice and care for them individually. He has to have a certain kindness in his heart for them, but he does not need to have any kind of a deep, intimate relationship with them. Therefore, the more priesthood is seen as simply ministry, the more celibacy for the priest will become suspect. By saying this, we are not saying ministry is bad, nor are we trying to make any critical comparisons with Protestant ministers. But the priest himself cannot help but make such comparisons, at least unconsciously. Why does his life style have to be so different when his life isn't? Aside from being needed to offer Mass or hear confessions, he often wonders what his real role is. Low morale is the predictable fallout.

It is also true that some priests may not be in direct ministry to people at all. They may spend their whole priestly life as part of the ecclesial bureaucracy, something on the order of middle managers in business. Since their concern is the smooth functioning of the institutional church, they may see no real need to have that type of relationship with their co-workers one would call "priestly." Without passing judgment on this situation, and assuming the priest has no other committed involvement in the church, it does make the necessity of living celibacy difficult to comprehend. Life and life style should be complementary.

A Call to Relationship

This returns us to the fundamental question: Is priesthood more than a ministry? Is it more than a function performed for the church? Building on the graces of confirmation, the sacrament of orders calls a priest to a unique sacramental relationship with that special and holy people we call the church. This requires that there must be something special going on between a priest and the faithful at a personal level. This is why it is important not to confuse doing priestly things with being a priest. After all, a couple need not be married to do married things. What makes the difference is the quality and depth of the relationship that exists between a husband and wife. It is no less important than the quality and depth of relationship that exists between a priest and his people. Doing "priestly things" has a hollow ring to it if the priest has no real relationship with his people. While a priest may be eager to point out this inconsistency in the case of a couple living together who do "married things," it may not be as easy for him to see or admit in his own case. Either he cannot see it because he regards priesthood as only a ministry, thus rendering unimportant his committed relationship to his people, or he prefers not to see it because it will mean a reevaluation of his life style.

A Priest's Changing Role

There is no question that the role of priests in the church is changing. Many people, both religious and lay, are performing functions once reserved to the priest alone. This is not just because they are often more competent or better qualified in certain areas of ministry, but also because it is their calling as adult Catholics. This is a welcome turn of events as the importance of confirmation is truly surfacing. While a priest is to be an overseer of these ministries, his unique role in this regard arises from something more than his being "head minister" or even the only minister in some areas of parish life. What a priest has to offer his people that no one else has to offer is the unique relationship he can have with them as their priest. Just as a couple's activity takes on a deeper significance and even a new meaning to the degree that there is genuine commitment and bonding between them, so priestly activity becomes truly "priestly" to the degree that it reflects a genuine commitment and bonding between himself and his people.

Enter celibacy. As a catalyst speeds up and enhances the chemical reaction of two elements without being essential to that reaction, the charism of celibacy deepens and enhances the relationship of the priest with his people without being essential to that relationship. From the nature of orders, celibacy alone is optional, not the intimacy of the priest-people relationship. Celibacy is meant to highlight the importance of this relationship and to facilitate its development and growth. Unless it is seen in this light, it will continue to be regarded like an inane Christmas gift: interesting, to be sure, but debatable as to actual identity or purpose.

An Unchanging Tradition

In those areas of a priest's life that cannot be performed by another person, like the celebration of the Eucharist, the relationship of the priest with his people has been recognized as a constant requirement throughout the history of the church. Father Peter Chirico, S. S., a Professor of Theology at St. Patrick's Seminary in Menlo Park, California, made the following observations on the critical shortage of priests:

> Liturgy is the celebration of the ultimate meaning of the whole life of the church. It brings that ultimate meaning to a focal expression. It is to the life of the church what sexual intercourse is to marriage. It is not an act that stands over and above and apart from life; rather, it springs from life, concentrates life, manifests what life means, and moves life forward.

Because liturgy is so connected with Christian life,
the participants in liturgy express therein the life-roles
they exercise. Hence, from earliest times, the bishop as
leader of the life of the church always presided at the
liturgy. He presided over liturgy because he presided
over life the same way that the president of the United
States presides over official state functions precisely
because he is the leader of the life of the political
community. In a parallel fashion, the leader of the
local community liturgy has been the leader of the
local community's Christian life.

This means that a priest cannot settle for being a good
provider for his parish any more than a father can settle for
being a good provider for his family. Celebrating the liturgy
is not a function he performs for his people, but rather a
celebration of the faith-community he enters into with his
people. This means the call for a priest, because he is a
priest, is to enter into the life of his people, to be a part of
them, not apart from them. Because he is the leader of the
community in worship, he is called also to be the leader of
the community's life. This requires entering into a depth of
relationship with the people on an ongoing basis.

Rather than being the operator of a spiritual filling sta-
tion, a priest is more like the conductor of an orchestra who
enables the talents of his people to emerge for the glory of
God. While ministering is going to be part of his role at
times, like helping the musicians with difficulties, his primary responsibility is the mission of recreating the music of
the Gospel. He is to bring together the often-dissonant
sounds of his people into the harmony of mutual coopera-
tion through love. He can do this because of his communion
with them. Rather than being above them, he is the center of
them. Similarly, a priest is like the father of a family. There
is value in what he does for his people, but it cannot replace
who he is with his people. Rather than being above them, he

is the center of them. This enables him to lead them by drawing out from them their gifts for the sake of building the Body of Christ and proclaiming the Gospel. The real issue here is not whether the priest is married or celibate, but whether or not he is living in a significant relationship with his people. The charism of celibacy has value on a day-to-day basis only to the extent that it facilitates such a relationship.

In other words, because a priest is neither married nor violating the demands of chastity, it does not mean, by these measures alone, that he is living the vow of celibacy at all. Celibacy cannot be understood in terms of what it is not, but only in terms of what it is. Celibacy is a charism of the Holy Spirit offered through the church to facilitate a genuine relationship of love between a priest and his people. This, in turn, sets the tone for the love relationship that should exist among the people of the church with one another.

2

Matrimony and Celibacy: Adversaries or Allies?

Before developing the nature of the charism of celibacy any further, it may be helpful to take a brief look at its history in the church. While this will be sketchy at best, the purpose in doing so is to reveal a rather intriguing discovery that surfaces along the way. Like a passenger on the bark of the church traveling down through time, celibacy had no idea that on that very same boat was a most unexpected fellow traveler, the sacrament of matrimony. In fact, they did not even meet for centuries. They had heard about each other, to be sure, but never in a way that would lead them to believe they had anything in common. They were obviously not booked in the same class at the beginning of their voyage. When they did meet, it seemed impossible that they would ever be friends. Part of their difficulty was an "identity crisis" that each suffered individually for centuries. Neither had any idea that they might eventually become so close that their very survival might depend on how they could draw strength from each other. It is only now that their identities are becoming clear. It is only now, at this point of their journey, that celibacy and the sacrament of matrimony are becoming aware of their mutual need for each other. It is only now that they are finding out they are traveling in the same class.

A Surprising History

Both celibacy and matrimony share a rather turbulent history in the church. Both have experienced forms of "seasick-
ness" as they have been at the mercy of unpredictable winds
and stormy seas. Even though both have roots in sacred
scripture, neither found full endorsement by the church until the latter part of the Middle Ages. In many ways, they
were victims of their times. For instance, the Council of
Nicea in 325 tried to prescribe celibacy as a universal church
law reflecting the influence of the prevalent Manichean heresy, which rejected the goodness of the human body, especially its sexual dimensions. Sex was seen as infected by sin
and, therefore, unbecoming for a priest. Fortunately, this
law was eventually rejected. In later centuries, celibacy became tangled up in controversies surrounding the church's
temporal concerns. Since priests were passing church prop-
erty on to their families, it was reasoned that forbidding
them to marry would stop this abuse. Imposing celibacy on
the clergy became the obvious strategy. Needless to say, such
reasons for celibacy were neither inspiring to hear nor in-
spired by the Gospel.

In fact, the Gospel presented celibacy in a positive light.
Its purpose and value was never for the sake of furthering
temporal causes but only for the sake of furthering the
Kingdom of God. In time, it became closely linked with the
monastic movement in the church, especially its ascetical
dimension. Eventually, celibacy for all priests, monastic and
otherwise, became the universal law of the church in the
twelfth century.[1] Unfortunately, this was in part a reflection
of the clear distinction that had evolved between the priestly
life and lay life, the former being regarded as "holier." The
understanding of celibacy was in a state of development.
Needless to say, it still had a way to go before being fully
appreciated.

It was at this time that the significance of the sacramental dimension of matrimony was beginning to emerge. Unfortunately, it too had reaped the unhealthy fruit of the Manichean heresy. If sex was bad, how could a married couple be a sign of Christ's love and a source of grace to the church? St. Augustine, who reflected this Manichean mentality, even linked sexuality with animality. The purpose of marriage was seen as limited to the begetting of children, literally born of his or her parents' "sin."[2] In the thirteenth century, however, the church found herself defending marriage and sexuality against the Albigensians. The most significant theologian of that time, St. Thomas Aquinas, saw that the sacramental gift of grace was related to the bond of love and accepted marriage unequivocally as part of the sacramental life of the church. He argued that God could not require sanctity in marriage without also supplying the means to achieve it.[3] Finally, in 1439, the Council of Florence officially declared matrimony as one of the seven sacraments of the church.

Roots in Scripture

With no desire to develop the often-murky details that flesh out the historical underpinnings for celibacy and matrimony, it is clear that the appreciation of their meaning and value was clearly evolutionary. Their full understanding still had a long way to go. Even though both are rooted in the Christian scriptures, neither was well understood over the years. Actually, celibacy was not linked to priesthood at all in the beginning, but to baptism, as an evangelical counsel that many in fact followed (cf. Matt. 19:10). Celibacy, as a dimension of the priestly state, was introduced only gradually and was ultimately based on the high value attached to virginity (cf. 2 Cor. 11:2; Eph. 5:25; Acts 21:9). This fact played a role in the struggle that marriage was to have in gaining its rightful place in the church. St. Paul's ambivalent view of marriage helped give rise to this situation. On the one hand, he saw marriage as a sign of Christ's union with his church (Eph. 5:21–33). But on the other, he seemed to wish that the faithful would renounce marriage in favor of virginity (1 Cor. 7:32–35). He gave the impression that marriage was secondary to virginity. Paul did so because he believed the second coming of Christ was imminent and was worried about married couples being too distracted with their responsibilities in the meantime. Making a living, caring for children, keeping house, for example, were just too demanding for the married to maintain the intense anticipation for Christ's return Paul deemed necessary. St. Paul did not say marriage was less important than virginity, but less important than the Second Coming. Nevertheless, the shadow was cast over marriage as a sanctifying state in life.

This shadow remained and even deepened over the centuries, which led to a distancing between celibacy and marriage in the process. Since celibates were the ones who were better educated, they were almost exclusively the ones who interpreted the writings of St. Paul and other sources on the subject. Even though much was written on marriage, celibacy seemed to get a lion's share of attention. While the glories of celibacy were proclaimed, comments on marriage were reduced pretty much to duties of the marital state in life from a celibate's perspective. Considering the weakness of human nature, it is not hard to see how an "I-am-better-than-you" mentality surfaced between these two ways of life. The common understanding of the faithful was that marriage was a lesser vocation. (This attitude prevails among many even into our own day.)

The Dawning of a New Day

This lengthening shadow reached all the way to the Council of Trent and subsequent canon law. It was not until the Second Vatican Council that this cloud, which in effect placed matrimony in the shadow of celibacy, was finally lifted. A new day dawned for the sacrament of matrimony when the bishops of the world said, "Authentic married love is taken up into divine love and is ruled and enriched by the redemptive power of Christ and the salvific action of the Church" (*Pastoral Constitution on the Church in the Modern World*, no. 48). There is no longer any reason for matrimonied couples to consider their state in life as a second-class vocation. In fact, as Father John T. Finnigan, former president of the Canon Law Society of America, notes: "When Christian marriage flounders, the witness of fidelity in all Christian vocations flounders."[4] This statement helps reveal that a true Christian marriage, which we recognize as a sacramental marriage in the Catholic Church, is more than a private affair between a husband and wife. As a sacrament, it involves the whole church.

This is a startling development of thought. In effect, it is saying that the sacrament of matrimony has a direct impact on the well-being of all the members of the church. Until this time, the sacrament had been looked upon as a private experience between husband and wife that the church blessed and thereby empowered so they could more faithfully bear up under the duties of the married state. But this is no longer adequate to describe this sacrament's purpose. The sacrament of matrimony is not just for the sake of the couple; it is also for the sake of the church. In fact, it offers a unique perspective for understanding the Gospel message itself. Whether dedicated singles or celibates, all who are baptized are called to a life of relationship in the church. This is integral to the Gospel and its full proclamation. As a truly ecclesial sacrament, matrimony holds out the image of how the faithful are to live out their commitments in the church. Matrimony also offers genuine hope that this is possible in a humanly fulfilling and joy-filled way. The church itself is "graced" by the sacramental couple.

Just from a human perspective, we can see why this is

true. Psychological studies show that people are inclined to live out the marriages of their parents in one way or the other. Children reflect the quality of their parents' marital relationship, for good or for ill. When the marital relationship is not strong, the children are more likely to have a problem with commitment in all areas of their lives. While such people may live up to their commitments, it is more apt to be in terms of an objective carrying out of responsibility. The humanness, warmth, and tenderness that can make it fulfilling are usually absent. On the other hand, children of parents with a strong relationship have a better chance at living out their commitments in a truly fulfilling way for themselves as persons.

For the Church

From an ecclesial perspective, the sacrament of matrimony is a commitment in faith that the couple make to the people of the church. The way couples live for the church will have an influence on how their brothers and sisters in the faith will live their lives of faith. Like yeast in dough, their sacramental presence among the faithful can have a leavening effect on the church. Their efficacy as a sacrament can bring about what they signify. They actually bring unity to a eucharistic celebration. The faithful can see the word of God, proclaimed from the pulpit, being lived in the flesh. This is especially true when couples have chosen to love each other beyond hurts and differences and when selfless love brings about reconciliation. All the faithful deserve to experience the married couples' sacramental love, beginning with their own children. When a sacramental couple love each other, the church herself becomes more loving.

Recent developments in sacramental theology support this understanding of matrimony. All of the sacraments are for the sake of the church, not just for the individuals who receive them. Yet, by and large, this communal aspect of the sacraments is poorly understood by the faithful. Too many still see sacraments only in terms of personal holiness, private experiences between themselves and God, without reference to the rest of the faithful. Many of the faithful simply do not see baptism as doing anything more than taking away original sin, reconciliation as anything more than removing sins, Eucharist as having any purpose other than personal sanctification.

In experiencing the love-relationship of sacramental couples, the call to a life of commitment to the community of the church through the celebration of all the sacraments becomes much clearer. And while celibacy is meant to facilitate the communal nature of orders, the sacrament of matrimony is emerging as an important support for celibacy, providing as it does an atmosphere of relationship in the church that makes a celibate priesthood easier to understand and live.

A Church Experience

While this is great news for matrimony and its rightful place as part of the church's sacramental treasury, it is not being embraced by everyone with open arms. Some married couples do not want to hear this "good news" simply because they do not want to be obligated to the church in any way. It is becoming more common to hear couples object to the church's teaching on divorce and remarriage, as though what they do with their lives is none of the church's business. Sadly, some even regard monogamy as an imposition on their lives much in the same way that many priests regard celibacy as an imposition on theirs. Clearly, these couples do not really see their marriages as sacramental, nor do they want to. They regard their marital relationship as a private matter that involves only themselves personally. They ignore entirely the ecclesial nature of their sacrament. They fail to acknowledge the distinction between marriage and matrimony: marriage being a holy covenant between the man and woman, and matrimony being a holy covenant between that couple and the people of the church. One is a private experience. The other is a church experience.

With this distinction, the meaning of fidelity in a sacramental marriage is expanded too. It is not just a matter that involves the relationship between a husband and wife but also their relationship with the people of the church. They have a responsibility to the faithful that is just as real as the one they have to each other. If a couple do not have this "sacramental sense," the other people of the church will simply be irrelevant to their lives as married couples. These are not bad people, they just have no sense of sacramental marriage. The church is not all that important to their life as a married couple. Ironically, they would never have considered being married anywhere else than in the church.

Two Attractive Options

Unfortunately, many priests as well seem to view the people of the church as irrelevant to their vow of celibacy. That is why it is good to remember that celibacy has been consistently linked to the church in one way or the other over the centuries, even though its understanding went through stages of evolution. But as the structures of the church evolved, so did the understanding of the Christian priesthood. It should not be surprising, therefore, that the relationship between celibacy and priesthood should evolve too. We are now at a time when they are actually seen as truly complementary to each other.

Priesthood, unlike matrimony, was always viewed as a sacrament for the church. Priests know that the sacrament of orders they receive on ordination day is not a private privilege for their own personal enjoyment. They know only too well that how they live their lives as priests will have a definite impact upon their people. This is why celibacy, a charism that facilitates the priest-people relationship, is such an important charism, not just for the priest but also for the people of the church. When the priest lives a life of committed love with his people, they will never question their worth or value in his eyes. Unfortunately, there are too many parishes where the people wonder why their priest is so distant. They cannot help but wonder what is wrong with them.

Whenever celibacy is viewed simply as the personal price one must pay to be ordained, its positive value is denied. It is absolutely imperative that a priest sees his priesthood as a call to a life of relationship with his people. Whatever the restrictions implied by celibacy, it is meant to encourage his relationship with his people. Lest we priests feel sorry for ourselves, this is not very different from the man who is expected to live a monogamous life with his wife because he marries in the church. Monogamy can be viewed as either a price to be paid or as a way of encouraging a depth of relationship with his wife to whom he is committing himself. Celibacy too must be looked upon positively if it is to be valued. Rather than just a requirement of law, it deserves to be viewed as the natural concomitant of the life of love that a priest and his people are to experience together. In other words, monogamy becomes a "problem" for a husband only when there is something wrong in his relationship with his wife. When all is well, anything else is unthinkable. It is similar with celibacy. When a priest is totally taken with his people, absorbed in them, then celibacy becomes "of course" instead of "I have to." It is only when this is understood that the issue of optional celibacy can be honestly discussed. Both matrimony and celibacy must be seen in a positive light or there is no real option at all. After all, a true option requires at least two attractive choices, not just one.

Other Christian Churches

It is now becoming more and more clear that neither matrimony nor celibacy is to be regarded as a private affair or life style. Of their nature, they are meant to be deliberately chosen church experiences. Without involving the people of the church, they make little sense. This awareness is not confined to the experience of the Catholic Church. Interestingly, those Christian churches that acknowledge matrimony as a sacrament also recognize its ecclesial dimension. For instance, the Anglican and Orthodox Churches see matrimony worthy of being listed with baptism and Eucharist as a sacrament of the church. Other Christian churches may regard marriage as a holy covenant, even worthy of reverence, but not worthy of equal status with the other sacraments. Furthermore, it is significant that only those Christian churches that acknowledge the sacramentality of matrimony also accept the sacramentality of priesthood. These same churches acknowledge the practice of celibacy as part of their clerical tradition. While they have not required celibacy for their priests in the same way the Roman Catholic Church has, they have accepted it as an optional life style worthy of support for the sake of the church.

It would be too easy to say this is just coincidental. There seems to be too close a connection between celibacy and the proclamation of matrimony as a sacrament. For instance, those churches that see matrimony as a sacrament also see and proclaim the beauty and value of celibacy as complementary to priesthood. It seems to be more than mere coincidence that churches that do not practice celibacy do not seem to have a full awareness of the beauty of marriage in the fullest Gospel sense either. At a recent Marriage Encounter national convention, where the sacramental vision of marriage was presented, a number of Protestant couples said they wished they too had the sacrament of matrimony in their churches. While they valued greatly their marriages, they began to see that the Gospel offered them a vision for their marriages that included the people of the church. This was a totally new awareness. In a sense, they reflected a feeling of disappointment that their churches did not give their marital relationship its full due. While marriage was proclaimed as a holy and sacred bond, it did not embrace the rest of the faithful. They wanted more. But while they were not thinking of it, their respective churches did not acknowledge any place for celibacy either.

Soon afterward, many of the same ideas about celibacy developed in this book were presented to joint gatherings of married couples and priests from across the country who worked in the church together. It was something like a test. Were the concepts "off the wall" or truly relatable to the lived experience of people who understood the values of relationship? The results were surprising and consistent. Even though the ideas were often totally new, they were received with genuine enthusiasm. They seemed to strike a responsive cord in both priests and couples. Not only did the priests begin to make more sense of the celibacy they were living, but married couples also began to understand its value for their lives. It was as if each group found an explanation for why they felt supported by the other when together. The love-relationship the couples were living with each other was nourishing the priests' efforts to live in relationship with their people. At the same time, the couples saw their love for each other in the ecclesial context. As celibate priests lived for the people of the church, the couples realized they had the same calling. Each had felt supported by the other and now could understand why. Matrimony could be fully appreciated only with celibate support, and celibacy could be fully understood only with the support of sacramental couples. Matrimony and celibacy are church experiences; they are complementary life styles meant for each other. If that is an overstatement, so be it, but there is certainly something positive going on between them.

Mutually Supportive

The point of all this is to show that the evolution of understanding of marriage and celibacy in the history of the church has brought them together in an extraordinary way. Rather than being at odds with each other, they are actually mutually supportive. Since priesthood has an ecclesial dimension, and since celibacy is meant to foster this dimension, underscoring the significance of relationship in the life of the priest, it becomes easier to recognize the significance of the ecclesial dimension of matrimony. Celibacy serves as a backdrop to the sacrament of matrimony, calling the couple to spend their love in a selfless way for the sake of the church, the Body of Christ. Celibate priests are in a unique position to empower couples to bring the special gifts born of their love into the very life of the church.

On the other hand, couples openly living the sacrament of matrimony call priests to a depth of relationship with their people they would find virtually impossible to consider otherwise. Sacramental couples provide an environment in the church that makes living celibacy more attractive and possible for the priest. He finds in the sacramental couple the kind of love he is to live with his people. But even more than that, he can draw on the grace of the sacrament of matrimony itself to empower him to live selflessly with his spouse, the church.

It is nothing short of an experience of grace to be with a husband and wife who continue to love each other beyond hurts and differences, not just for their own sakes, but also for the sake of the church. Take the case of the couple who had a fight just before going to bed. In anger, the husband took his blanket and pillow and retreated to the living-room couch. After a few minutes of smoldering, the thought struck him, "We are a sacrament of the church, and our people deserve more from us than this." With that, he returned to the bedroom, expressed his sudden awareness to his wife, and they spent the next couple of hours healing their hurt before going to sleep.

Any priest who hears this story cannot help but be impressed by the faith being lived out by this couple. He cannot help but hear the call in his own heart to heal his relationship with some people in his own parish, people he feels like writing off. Clearly, he is being called to a depth of relationship with them he cannot ignore any longer. This is good news for priests who think they always have to be in the giving role. They have so much to receive from faithful couples. But it is also good news for married couples to know they have so much to give.

The intimate connection between matrimony and celibacy really highlights the connection between the two sacraments of matrimony and priesthood. They support each other as true ecclesial vocations. But if this connection is not acknowledged, the church itself suffers. Again, those faith-communities that do not acknowledge the vocational nature of matrimony and priesthood in the church regard baptism alone as the ecclesial vocation. The richness and power of sacramental relationships is absent or at least is not formally recognized or proclaimed. Furthermore, when celibacy is not valued, the values of relationship are not as loudly proclaimed either. This affects married couples and their sense of value as a sacrament proclaiming the value of relationship to the church. In turn, this deprives priests of a vital sign needed for the fulfillment of their call to live in relationship with their people. It is a vicious circle.

A Lived Experience

As noted above, the evidence to support this is not found in some theological treatise, but in the life experiences of priests and couples. Loving couples have helped countless priests live out their personal commitments. Actually, the beautiful thing about a loving couple is that at the center of their existence is their love for each other — a man loving a woman, a woman loving a man. They define themselves in terms of that love. That is precisely what a priest must do. Rather than define himself in terms of what he does for his people, like being a good provider, he must define himself in terms of his love for his people, both men and women. A priest is meant to be one who is passionately in love with his people. His whole life is to be centered around his relationship with his people. The focus of his life cannot be in terms of his professional competencies, as helpful as they may be, or even his accomplishments, but in terms of how close he is to his people. Just as a husband, as husband, can be identified only in terms of his wife, so a priest, as priest, can be identified only in terms of his people.

To put this another way, because of celibacy, many priests have a greater appreciation of the sacrament of matrimony and how the witness of the couple's love for each other and the church is calling them to be more loving with their people. Celibacy is a reminder to couples that they should never have to live their vocation alone. They have the church to support and guide them. And because of the sacrament of matrimony, many married couples have a greater appreciation of celibacy. Without the witness of celibate priests, matrimonied couples would be lacking a powerful reminder that their love is not just for themselves but also for the sake of the faithful. Matrimony is a living reminder to priests that celibacy is not a sentence to loneliness but a call to unconditional love and communion.

Unfortunately, there is another lived experience that most of us priests are more familiar with. Because so much of our pastoral time is spent trying to help people who are hurting, we experience the consequences of unhappy marriages more than we do those of happy ones. We experience the anger of women who have been hurt by men. Albeit secondhand, we receive its sting. For this reason, many of us become protective of our masculinity by becoming hard-nosed. Add to this the anger of unhappy religious sisters and single women in the church, which is often directed our way as a symbol of "the church," and we begin to see why some of us at times become embarrassed by our own masculinity and even run away from it. If for no other reason, this underscores the need for priests to have solid relationships with happily married couples. We need to be helped by husbands as well as wives: husbands who understand a woman's heart and really love their wives, and wives who truly trust their husbands as men and openly love them. We need this to balance out the negative experiences we must deal with almost daily. In some ways, the celibate-matrimony connection can be a matter of survival, but it is meant to be so much more.

A Negative Witness

In a negative sort of way, this unlikely connection between matrimony and celibacy is evident all around us today. Marriage is going through tough times in the church right along with celibacy. While unhappy celibates are looking for intimacy, unhappily married couples, not finding it in their lives, are looking for independence. In both cases, the search is for an intimacy they are not experiencing. The irony in this should not be lost. When marriage is not lived, it is every bit as unfulfilling as celibacy when it is not lived. To blame either the nature of celibacy or marriage would be foolish.

Truly, the relationship between the two is extraordinary. Considering current trends, one wonders if they are not destined to rise and fall together. While it is cause of great concern that some 25 percent of the priests in our country have left the priesthood since the early 1960s, it is no less tragic that close to half the marriages celebrated this year in the United States will end in divorce. Much to our chagrin, divorces in the Catholic Church are keeping pace with the national average. This situation is enough to make one wonder how many priests who leave to marry do so because they find marriage so overwhelmingly attractive or celibacy so overwhelmingly grating. While it is easy to romanticize about marriage, priests as well as anyone know the shape it is in. It is not an exaggeration to say that marriage has never seemed less attractive than it does today. Married couples are finding it unattractive, and priests know it. One cannot help wonder if some priests are not marrying to get away from something more than to enter into a committed love-relationship. Like entering a marriage on the rebound, it is a dangerous position to be in.

It would seem to be a mistake, therefore, to address the state of celibacy as a separate phenomenon from the state of matrimony. Again, they seem to be intimately linked. Together, they are reeling from the shock waves of a society that has turned its back on the very notion of commitment itself. "Why be committed to anything or anyone?" "What's in it for me?" "If priests can break their vows, why can't we?" Twenty years ago, it was shocking to hear about a Catholic couple divorcing or a priest leaving the priesthood to marry. While it may still be sad to hear today, it is no longer shocking.

Perhaps celibacy is caught in the backwash of what is happening on a broader scale to marriage. Because of the pressure on matrimony, celibacy is under attack too. There does not seem to be that sea of matrimonial love in the church needed to support the values of committed relationship that a celibate must have if he is to survive. After all, he can tread water only so long. This correlation between the quality of the sacrament of matrimony and the quality of celibacy should not be taken lightly. If matrimony does not receive the support it deserves in our church today, priests themselves will experience the unhappy consequences. Conversely, if celibacy is not supported by married couples, they too will experience unhappy consequences in their lives.

A Matter of Concern

Since the need for intimacy between celibate priests and married couples will benefit both, what is happening to each of them today must be taken seriously. The breakdown of marriage in both society and the church cannot be just a matter of passive interest to celibate priests. It will have a direct impact on their lives sooner or later. Ironically, it is in the priests' own interest, not to mention the interest of the hierarchy, that they support the renewal of the sacrament of matrimony currently underway in the church. By the same token, matrimonied couples stand to lose if the charism of celibacy is lost as a gift of the Spirit for the sake of the church. As living sacraments, they deserve to hear the call from their priests to look beyond themselves to those in the church who desperately need to see their other-centered love. Their lives proclaim that this kind of love is not only possible but also that it works.

Celibacy and matrimony have traveled a long way together over the centuries. Considering the journey that lies ahead, it is imperative that they realize they are not adversaries at all. They are gifts of the church, for the church, whose future is one they seem to be destined to share together, one way or the other. How they were treated in the past may be cause for discouragement, even scandal. But those responsible for it then can always plead ignorance. The way matrimony and celibacy will be treated in the future, however, is in our hands today. Whether we like it or not, we are traveling with them at this moment in history. The winds are still unpredictable. The sea is still stormy. The least we can do is to look carefully at them before passing judgment on their relevance in our modern world. We know things about them today never realized before in the church. Some of it even speaks to the deepest longings of the human heart. If, by indifference or a lack of openness, we frustrate their apparent emergence as gifts for the life of the church whose time has come, what will we plead?

3

Bachelor or Bridegroom?

It is difficult for many to think of celibacy in a positive light. This is understandable since so many negative things have been said about it in the past several years, as well as the sobering impact of the number of respected men who have left the priesthood to marry. In fact, when someone is overheard speaking about celibacy in a positive way, the conditioned reaction for many is to excuse that person as an uninformed member of the church, or as one who is clearly self-righteous, hopelessly conservative, or unwilling to bend with the fresh breezes of change. It is as if all that needs to be said on the issue has been said, and now it is time for the institutional church to catch up with reality. Unfortunately, when feelings run high like this, they may drown out those voices trying to speak to the positive value of celibacy as a charism of the church. For this reason, it is important to remember that this discussion is on the nature of celibacy itself; it is not a defense of church law. In other words, the law of celibacy is not to be confused with the charism of celibacy. This is why the following questions must be asked: If celibacy has a place in the church, what is it? If celibacy is ever to be an option for a priest, what is that option all about?

Optional Celibacy

Reflecting on what has been said already, it may be becoming clear that celibacy should be optional in the Catholic Church. On closer examination, however, we discover it already is. Optional celibacy is not something we need wait for. Priests have the option to choose or not choose a celibate way of life today. And this choice is not between celibacy and a priest's leaving the priesthood to get married, or even living in the shadows of the infamous "third way." (The "third way" refers to a priest secretly having a wife or mistress.) The reason this is true is because the opposite of celibacy is not marriage but bachelorhood. After all, a bachelor is identified simply as one who is not married. He is not committed to anyone in a deeply personal and permanent way. His life is his own, free of binding relationships. He is known for his independence.

Celibacy is a charism of relationship, not a sentence to loneliness. Of its nature, it has far more in common with married people than anyone else. That is why, if the church were to impose a life of nonmarriage on her priests, and that was all there was to it, it would be sinfully oppressive. It would be a denial of his basic humanity. Besides, the very nature of priesthood calls for a binding relationship of a priest with his people. It would be a contradiction in terms to ask a man to be a priest and then expect him to live as a bachelor. A priest cannot be simply described as a "man of God." He is more than that. He is a "man of God's people." He is not somehow suspended between God and his people. He lives within the community of God's people and discovers God with them.

Celibacy is a charism that enables a priest to commit himself to a way of loving for life. It is not an excuse to run away from people, to hide from people, or to look down on people. As a gift of the Spirit through the church, it is not something that fights against human nature. On the contrary, it enables the priest to live a full life and to overcome the pitfalls of loneliness and isolation. When living in relationship with his people, his basic human emotional needs for love, belonging, self-worth, and autonomy will be met. He is no less a man because he is celibate. In fact, his masculinity is a critical factor in the way he lives out his commitment with his people. There is no need to feel sorry for a priest who is drawing on the grace of this charism.

When some men choose to leave the priesthood to marry, they often proclaim their need for relationship and their human need for intimacy. It would be foolish to argue with this fact. But it would be equally foolish to try to prove that the only way a person can live a full human life is by being married. This is why it is nothing short of irony that the most effective support emerging for a celibate priest to live a full and rewarding relationship with his people comes from married couples themselves.

In many ways this is a hard saying, since it contradicts the impression given by some who leave the priesthood to marry. They occasionally imply that those who remain are condemned to unfulfilled lives, if not to lives that are actually destructive to their humanity. Unfortunately, many lay people have accepted this as fact, honestly believing that it is not only unhealthy for a priest to be celibate (read: unmarried), but also impossible for him to live it (read: avoid sexual involvement with women or possibly men). It is not surprising, therefore, that people are open to having a married clergy. They love their priests and do not think the sacrifices priests are asked to make in their behalf are justified. It is not uncommon for people to say, "What a waste of a good man." But hearing this over and over again does not offer much support to the average priest. There is just something about knowing people feel sorry for you that plays havoc with your sense of dignity and self-esteem as a man, not to mention as a priest. Sometimes it is even worse than that. It is devastating when a priest catches a suspicious look that proclaims actual disbelief that he is living a chaste life. It may not happen all that often, but it hurts and leaves a lasting impression. This does not imply that celibate priests are above such sins. Unquestionably, there were priests in the crowd who humbly walked away from the woman caught in adultery when Jesus said, "Let the man among you who has no sin be the first to cast a stone at her" (John 8:7). What hurts here is the clear insinuation that such sinful liaisons are cynically accepted to be a way of life for many priests, at least those who are "with it." For the faithful to be open to a married clergy may well be a good thing, but only if it is for the right reasons. Feeling sorry for their celibate priests is not one of them.

Turning the Corner

Since the task of developing a positive attitude about celibacy seems like such an uphill struggle, where does one begin? Keeping in mind the marriage-celibacy connection, it may be good to start by trying to understand the richness of the marital relationship when it is being lived fully. This means avoiding those who see marriage as their "profession." Contrary to popular opinion, a movie star who has been married several times is not the expert on marriage we are looking for. "Professions" are just too easy to change. Such a person eventually becomes only an expert on divorce. The expert on marriage must always remain an "amateur," that is, one who stays involved because of love. This is the one who marries once, is committed to it, and lives it to the full. Fortunately, there are many such experts in the church for us to reflect on. Their marriages are the kind that will guide our examination of celibacy.

A Divine Paradigm

People get married because they want to. It is not imposed from on high. When God said to Adam, "It is not good for the man to be alone" (Gen. 2:18), he was saying that he created the man incomplete. A man cannot live a full life by himself. He needs another who will complement, even complete, him as a human being. It is equally true to say that it is not good for the woman to be alone either. She too is incomplete and turns to the man to complement, even complete, her as a human being. In other words, they were both created, predisposed, "programed," if you will, for relationship. When a man and woman choose to marry, it is because they want to find a fuller, more complete life with their spouse. "That is why a man leaves his father and mother and clings to his wife, and the two of them become one body" (Gen. 2:24). This is not a put-down of parents; it just says the parent-child relationship is not enough to meet the needs of an adult man or woman.

There is something deep within the human spirit that calls us as human beings to one another. In this sense, God did not create a man and a woman as much as he created man/woman. He did not set out to create individuals. He wanted to create community. He created human beings for one another. Such is the nature of the human creation. From a diversity of persons comes unity. The man and the woman become "one body" (Gen. 2:24). This is not unlike the very nature of the Trinity itself. From a diversity of persons, Father, Son, and Spirit, there is but one God. How two totally different persons can be one in marriage is no less a mystery than how three totally different persons can be one God.

The three persons of the Trinity are absolutely different. Their unity comes from the absolute love that each person of the Trinity has for each other person, as is. Furthermore, the nature of this love is intimacy, not benevolence (doing good). The marital relationship of man and woman finds its paradigm in this divine love relationship. While the man and woman are distinct persons, the nature of their committed, unconditional, exclusive love for each other, as is, is also their unity. As in God, this is the love of intimacy, not benevolence. The married couple, in turn, is an image of the divine paradigm for the human community. From the diversity of persons in the human family can come unity when love is operative among them. Again, a benevolent love is not enough. Intimacy is called for.

When people ask about the meaning of life, this is part of the answer. Life is about community. Life is about love between people who are different from one another. Life is about persons belonging to other persons. All claims of American society to the contrary, the glory of the individual alone is not what life is all about. Living in splendid isolation from others is a violation of human nature. Rather than revealing the wonder of God, individualism obscures it.

Living in community is only part of the meaning of life because there is more to the Trinity than three distinct persons living in unity. They are also generative. Not only did they create everything by the power of their mutual love, they continue to sustain everything in creation by their mutual love. It was not just by divine whim that God commanded the first man and woman to "Be fertile and multiply" (Gen. 2:28). He was empowering them to image for the world something essential for living a full human life. Regardless of one's state in life, all people are called to be generative of life by their love for one another and to sustain that new life by their continuing love. Human life is about intimacy and generativity. It is about what God is about, nothing more, nothing less. The human community takes its cue for living from the image of God it has in the married couple. So too does the celibate priest.

Matrimony: A Celibate's Guide

Therefore, people get married in order to satisfy those needs deep within them that are meant to be met in the context of a committed relationship: the need to be loved, to belong, the need for self-worth and autonomy. In fact, people should not be frightened when they experience negative feelings that say these needs are not being met. Such feelings are God's way of calling them to enter into or to go back to their committed relationships with others.

If we are not careful here, however, it would appear that getting married is a rather self-centered, even selfish thing to do, as if the focus of the whole experience is on oneself. There are, no doubt, many who would support this "what's-in-it-for-me" mentality. But, ironically, the exact opposite seems to be the lived experience of those couples who find their marriages most fulfilling. Their attention is not on themselves but on their spouse. The dynamic between the bride and groom makes this most evident. In giving himself unreservedly to his bride, the groom is open to receive his beloved. In offering herself to her beloved, the bride experiences the joy of being loved. Because of their love for each other, the groom is willing to place himself in the hands of his bride. He is willing to let his beloved form and shape him, so generous is his act of self-giving. He is not afraid of losing his identity. On the contrary, he knows he will be more complete as a man because of his unconditional love. His identity will become even more evident.

A Groom's Love

The extraordinary thing about a bridegroom is that he is not concerned with himself. He is totally absorbed in his bride. She is all that matters. He is ready to lose himself in her by being totally responsive to her. He will measure his success as a husband by how his wife experiences him. Contrary to modern theory, he will not measure his success by what he gets out of the marriage for himself. What will his bride get out of their relationship because of his love for her? That is his primary concern. He has eyes only for her. While this may change as time goes by because of unhealed hurts or taking each other for granted, it is the furthest thing from a groom's mind when he sees his bride walking down the aisle. This is because he is caught up in the wonder of love.

It is only when a groom's love for his wife begins to die that he will begin to look inward and wonder what is in it for himself. It is at that moment that justice replaces love as the guiding principle of his relationship with his wife. No longer does either feel inclined to give 100 percent to their relationship. Their marriage becomes a fifty fifty proposition. Both begin to measure each other on how well they are living up to the "bargain." What was once full starts becoming empty. What was celebrated in intimacy starts being lived in loneliness. The groom's measure of success then becomes how satisfied he is. But that was not the way he saw reality when his love was fresh and alive. He would be the first to admit that when their love was strong, he found his satisfaction in doing all he could to satisfy her. She was his life.

We must be careful not to give into the cynicism that says love is blind and he'll get over it. It would also be too easy to pass off a groom's enthusiasm for his bride as the result of overactive hormones, his and hers. While it is unrealistic to expect the honeymoon to last forever, it is not unrealistic to think the man and woman may have found a valid and meaningful expression of the myth that is deep within them. Who is to say they have not discovered a unity with each other they had not thought possible? And this unity came from self-giving to another, not from self-seeking. When St. Paul said, "Husbands should love their wives as they do their own bodies" (Eph. 5:28), he was simply urging them to pursue that depth of intimacy open to them. Why should they settle for less?

But is it supposed to last, this unity of love born of selfless giving? Why not? St. Paul also said, "Husbands, love your wives, as Christ loved the Church. He gave himself up for her to make her holy" (Eph. 5:25). Jesus lived out the fullness of who he was by faithfully giving himself totally to his beloved, the church. The constant reminder of this kind of faithful giving is the way a husband gives himself totally to his wife for her sake, "to make her holy," to help her grow to the fullness of life. Since holiness is closely related to wholeness, to the complete integration of a person through the power of love at work, and since such growth does not happen overnight, there is no question that the unity a couple experience early in marriage is meant to last. More than that, it is meant to deepen. It would be foolish to expect a coupled married for thirty years to love each other as honeymooners. They have been through too much together. They know each other's flaws and weaknesses too well. This is why their love is meant to be deeper. It can be just as romantic as before, maybe even more so. But now they love each other as they really are, just like Jesus loves us as we really are. (Unfortunately, too many couples claim their love is too "mature" to be romantic. This is probably just an excuse for their lack of intimacy.)

The Giving Paradox

We are dealing with a paradox here. In giving we somehow receive. Jesus put it this way, "Give, and it shall be given to you. Good measure pressed down, shaken together, running over, will they pour into the fold of your garment. For the measure you measure with will be measured back to you"

(Luke 6:38). While this text is usually used to make a case for tithing to the church, its context is Luke's great discourse on love. Applying it here, this paradox becomes evident because a husband knows he can best meet his need to be loved by loving his wife. When a husband feels the need to be loved, it is not enough for him to throw out hints of his need to his wife with the hope she will respond by showing love in return. To receive love, he must make the decision to love. Similarly, should his wife feel lonely and thereby realize her need to belong is not being met, it is time for her to choose to love beyond the hurts and pains that exist in her relationship with her husband. She is responsible to make a positive effort to get her need for belonging met. Being passive just does not work. She must initiate the reaching out.

This same paradox holds true when a spouse's self-esteem is wanting. The temptation for many is to compensate for what is lacking by getting busy and accomplishing something worthwhile, like increasing job performance or getting involved in civic activities or absorbing oneself in raising the kids. This strategy of compensation is often used when one substitutes gaining respect for being loved, or power over people for belonging to them. Unfortunately, such efforts become addictive and consequently less satisfying as time goes by. Unhappily, they can anesthetize a couple to the initial warnings that they are beginning to drift apart. Granted, efforts at compensation may smother those feelings that indicate the poor self-esteem, but at best they are only a short fix, since they do not address the real issue: the condition of the relationship between wife and husband. That is where the effort needs to be directed.

A devoted husband struggling with his self-esteem, rather than focusing attention on himself, turns his attention to his spouse. He realizes he is part of something bigger than himself. Therefore, instead of waiting for his wife to sense how he feels, he reaches out to her and affirms her. When she is feeling good about herself, he will experience his own self-worth in return, "good measure, pressed down, shaken together, running over." In giving he receives. This is his free choice. He does not reach out to his beloved because he has to or even because he should. He reaches out because he wants to. He loves her. That is his motive.

Freedom of Choice

A devoted husband is not forced to love his wife. Love cannot be forced. It is always a free choice, or it isn't love at all. It may not always be a pleasant choice or a joyful choice, but it is always a free choice. If this were not true, spouses would feel trapped in their relationships. Consequently, their basic human emotional need for autonomy could not be met. Free choice must always be part of any healthy relationship.

The much sought-after sense of personal freedom comes from taking responsibility for one's life in the context of one's freely chosen commitments. For the married, it does not come from living independently from one's spouse. Autonomy is not the freedom to live life without commitments but rather the freedom to live those commitments fully. It is worth remembering here that this is not some rule imposed on married people by church law. It arises from the very nature of their being human. It is the way they were "programed" from the beginning. Ironically, those who choose a life of independence often find themselves very lonely at the same time. It is not good for the man or the woman to be alone. But a fulfilling relationship does not just happen. The couple must make it happen by choosing to give themselves to each other without reserve.

A Celibate's Needs

It is a little disconcerting when people announce with a sense of genuine discovery that they met a priest who was a "real human being." It would be fascinating to know what they thought before experiencing such a revelation. Priests have the same basic human emotional needs as all other normal men, needs that can be satisfied only in a committed relationship with others: for love, belonging, self-esteem, and autonomy. The charism of celibacy is to facilitate such relationships and to help priests meet these fundamental needs. It should be noted, however, that genital sex is not such a need. It is a want. Some, of course, will debate this. But the evidence of sacred scripture, the tradition of church teaching for 2,000 years, and the lived experience of countless saints of history and of ordinary people of today cannot be ignored just because we are living in a sexually compulsive society.

Tragically, genital sex has been dehumanized in our society to the point that it has been reduced to little more than an animal activity (Manacheanism revisited?). It is the human factor in genital sex that gives it its full meaning. Without the presence of genuine love, sexual activity is simply exploitation (read: "scoring"); without expressing the commitment to belong, it is common fornication; without respecting self-worth, it is an act of abuse; and without free choice, it is rape. To offer as a defense, "But I needed it!" has the empty ring of a cymbal clashing and gong booming.

Sexual intimacy for the married couple expresses love, belonging, self-worth, and autonomy because of the unique nature of their relationship. It is that unique relationship they have that makes genital sex a "need" for them. But the human emotional needs for love, belonging, self-worth, and autonomy are common to all people at all stages of life. It would be unthinkable to believe God would not provide ways for these needs to be met other than in genital sex.

There is an interesting paradox here. It is when these four basic human emotional needs are respected that sexual intimacy is humanly fulfilling for the married couple. Similarly, it is when these four human emotional needs are met that celibate intimacy is humanly fulfilling for a priest. Without going into it, it is the exclusivity of the husband-wife relationship that frees them to take full responsibility for the consequences of their genital expressions of love. This is simply not possible for a celibate, as he is committed to a nonexclusive love. There is no way he could be free to accept the consequences of genital love-making. Nonetheless, celibates and other singles in the church can celebrate true love in other meaningful and satisfying ways in keeping with the nature of their relationships in the church and society.

The Celibate Bridegroom

When a man is ordained to the priesthood, he is making a positive choice to dedicate himself totally to the Body of Christ. This is just as real a choice as a groom makes when he dedicates himself totally to his bride. In response to God's grace, a priest makes a full commitment in love to the people of the church for their happiness and fulfillment, not his. Being caught up in the wonder of selfless love, he is not worried about himself. He just knows his basic human emotional needs for love, belonging, self-esteem, and autonomy will somehow be satisfied. He is not taking a job. He is taking a bride. She is all that matters. Like a bridegroom, the priest is caught up in the paradox of giving. For this reason, a priest in a very special way is an *alter Christus*, another Christ.

One of the most precious titles Jesus called himself was a bridegroom. Fundamentally, a priest is to be a bridegroom to his people, utterly absorbed in and responsive to them.

The real issue about celibacy is not what the priest gets out of it. It is not for himself. It is for his people. How are they affected by his celibacy? That is the issue. The focus of his celibacy is not what he has given up, but the church, his people, to whom he has committed himself in love. The measure of his success as a priest will be in terms of what his spouse experiences from him. When he offers himself totally to the church on his ordination day, his own heart is filled. Such is the dynamic of love.

This does not say that celibacy is essential to priesthood, but it does say celibacy is a valid, beautiful, and important charism in the church for the sake of the church (read: people, not institution). It can be understood only in terms of a love commitment to the Body of Christ and not in terms of what has to be sacrificed in order to live it. Being a celibate priest calls for a love relationship as much as being a husband or wife, son or daughter, brother or sister, a father or mother. It has to be judged and approached on these terms. While all of these relationships require the fulfilling of duties, personal integrity, and living up to responsibilities, the real test is how the people, husband and wife, etc., live with each other. The test of celibacy is whether or not the priest is involved with his people in a celibate way. This cannot be evaluated by how well he functions or how efficiently he gets things done. Celibacy is a matter of the heart, and the celibate will know the answer by what is going on inside him. He will be living celibacy when his needs for love, belonging, self-esteem, and autonomy are being satisfied in his relationship with his people.

A Giving Heart

Like any bridegroom, a true celibate has a giving heart. When he senses a need in himself to be loved, he must reach out in love to his people. He cannot passively sit back and wait for them to come to him. He must take responsibility for meeting his needs, and he does so by giving of himself. When he feels a distance from his people, he knows he must love beyond any pains and hurts between himself and them. This may mean asking for forgiveness from the pulpit or renewing his efforts to love those who are unattractive and difficult to love (read: those who generally disagree with him). He need not fear those negative feelings that signal these unmet needs, like loneliness or even anger. They are God's beckoning him to a better relationship with his people. Besides, his people, the Body of Christ, cannot afford to have him withdraw from them to a life of independence. Not only does he need them, they also need him as well.

Like any married person, a priest must fight those temptations to compensate for his unmet needs. It is so easy for a priest to distance himself from his people by becoming needlessly busy. It is so easy to substitute respect for love and power for intimacy. It is so easy for a priest to become a bachelor rather than a bridegroom. Fighting the seductive attractiveness of independence will be his constant struggle. In its tradition, the church has allowed both a married and celibate clergy, but never a bachelor clergy. Somehow it just seems to jeopardize too much the sacredness of the relationship of a priest with his people. Somehow it blurs too much the sign of Christ the bridegroom whom the priest has the privilege of being with his spouse, the faithful of the church. In its inwardness, bachelorhood seems to violate too much the spirit of a giving heart.

When his own self-esteem is at stake, it is difficult for a lonely priest not to pull rank. There is truth to the charge, noted previously in chapter 1, that loneliness leads to "cynicism, arbitrary authoritarianism, clinical aloofness or various forms of escapism including dependency on alcohol and drugs." But this does not mean that the only alternative is to leave the priesthood to marry. There is the option of living the charism of celibacy. A disillusioned priest, like a disillu-

sioned husband, can choose to rekindle the dream that mo-
tivated him to give himself totally to his spouse on his day of
ordination. He can choose to refocus his attention on his
beloved people by loving beyond his hurts and disappoint-
ments. When his sense of self-esteem is wanting, a priest can
remember that he is part of something bigger than himself
and can choose to affirm, praise, and build up his spouse,
the people of the church. When he finds them feeling better
about themselves, he will experience his own self-worth in
return. While there are many options open to the priest,
choosing to live as a bridegroom is one of them. The real
question is how much does he want to? His life and the life
of the church are at stake.

Choosing Celibacy

A celibate priest cannot be forced to love his people. It must
be his choice, because love cannot be forced. This means
that celibacy itself must be a free choice each priest has to
make in the context of his own life with his people. It may
not be a pleasant choice or a joyful choice at times, but it is
always a free choice. If this were not true, a priest could not
meet his need for autonomy in his relationship with his
people. Nor could he have a truly healthy relationship with
them. When a priest feels "trapped" in the priesthood because of a law of celibacy he does not choose, his people
will pick it up. They can often sense something is wrong but
not know what it is. In not choosing celibacy, a priest in
effect, is choosing not to give himself to his people fully.
Psychologically, this is why many of the faithful feel be-
trayed, as if they have gone through a divorce, when their
priest leaves them "for another woman." Again, the similar-
ity with matrimony is striking.

This is why the misunderstandings that surround the

whole question of celibacy are so devastating to the church in our day. Some priests are angry because they hear only a law of the institutional church saying they cannot get married. This makes it almost impossible for them to hear the call from the people of the church inviting them to live a life of intimacy and belonging with them. A priest who does not have a sense of freedom in his celibacy often withdraws in rebellion and anger. In turn, this makes the lure of a bachelor life style an attractive option to him. But living in anger is not a very positive response to the problem. It can cause an ongoing stress that may affect his physical health. Worse still, living in isolation from his people will not satisfy his basic emotional needs as a healthy human being.

While it may look like a good option at the time, living separately is not one that embraces the hopes and dreams the priest had when he was ordained. In fact, if he had envisioned his living eventually as a bachelor back then, one cannot help but wonder if he would have chosen to be ordained in the first place. Living as a bachelor may protect a priest from being bothered by his people, but that does not say much for the excitement and love he has for them. It may bring peaceful coexistence, but peaceful coexistence is no more acceptable in the church between priest and people than it is between husband and wife. It is settling for less than the call of the Gospel: "Love one another, as I have loved you" (John 15:21).

4

Masculine, Feminine, or Neuter?

In the last chapter we said that a priest is no less a man because he is celibate. It will be the aim of this chapter to go even a step further. The charism of celibacy serves to enhance the masculinity of a priest and, it should be added, the femininity of a religious woman. Needless to say, this is not a self-evident truth. (What is said here, while focusing on priests, could be applied equally as well to women, and should be.) The popular opinion, if not the wish of many, seems to be that celibates should be more neuter than anything else. They are to play down their masculinity and femininity as much as possible. After all these years, it is not hard to find people who still believe that human sexuality is something that should not interfere with the work of God. (The ghost of the Manicheans lives!)

The fear of one's masculinity worked its way into the training of many a priest. "Sexuality" and "priesthood" were almost mutually exclusive terms. Many seminarians received the impression that sexual feelings had no place in their lives and that they should be suppressed. Apparently a holy priest should not have such feelings either. Priests were to be men in every way but sexually, whatever that meant. The frequent reminder heard in seminaries that "there was no such thing as a wooden Indian" (read: when around women your sexual feelings may be stirred) served as a warning to future priests to keep women at a safe distance. The law of celibacy served to reinforce this warning with the weight of the whole church. Not only would closeness to women be a violation of one's priestly lifestyle, it could also jeopardize his very standing with the church.

This is to question neither the good faith, noble intentions, nor positive contributions of those who were responsible for seminary training twenty-five years ago. If they had had available to them the fruits of the scholarly research that have brought many new insights to our understanding of human psychology and development that are available today, most would have been eager to adapt seminary practices accordingly. Their first concern was to prepare men for the priestly life in the world as they understood it. Current priestly formation programs do take this material into account. But our point here is not to evaluate seminary training; it is to try to understand better the concept of celibacy as it relates to a priest's masculinity.

Since we are saying celibacy is a charism of relationship, and not a tool to reinforce a "safe" distance between a priest and his people, two questions in need of an answer come to mind: What are those awarenesses that have changed our understanding of celibacy? What does celibacy have to do with them?

Male and Female

We also mentioned in the last chapter that the climax of the first biblical story of creation was the creation of the man/woman. "In the divine image he created him, male and female he created them" (Gen. 1:27). Together, in their shared humanity, Adam and Eve reflected the image of the divine. This means, of course, that the divine nature itself was capable of being expressed with both male and female qualities. In the second story of creation (Gen. 2:5–25), a further awareness surfaces. There was a certain "incompleteness" about the man without a "suitable partner for him." But as this story unfolds we see that God creates the woman from the man, not separately, as it were, apart from him. "The Lord God then built up into a woman the rib that he had taken from the man" (Gen. 2:22). We can infer from this that the original man, Adam, had both male and female qualities. That is, the man had within himself those qualities that would eventually be identified as feminine. It is not unreasonable to assume that the woman, "taken from the man," shared a dual sexuality as well. Since she was taken from the man, she had something masculine within her. Clearly, unlike their Creator, neither the man nor the woman was "complete" in himself/herself.

We may conclude that not only was the man not meant to be alone but also that neither was the woman. Each had some inner need for the other for completeness. While this scriptural text is certainly not meant to withstand scientific scrutiny, the story as told implies there is something about the psychology of a man that calls out for a feminine influence in his life. At the same time, there is something about a woman that calls out for a masculine influence in her life. Without that feminine influence, a man's masculinity could not fully develop. Similarly, without that masculine influence, a woman's femininity could not fully develop either. Since, according to the story of Genesis, the destiny of Adam and Eve was to "become one body," it becomes imperative for the man and woman to work together toward unity in their life. To the degree they succeed, to that degree will they find their "completeness" as persons.

While this may appear to be reading an awful lot into the story of creation, it is very possible that when the author of Genesis wrote the story, he did so with the awareness of other traditions that saw the original human being as both male and female. For instance, this notion appeared in both Persian and Talmudic mythologies. Even Plato tells a fascinating Greek myth about how the original human beings were round spheres with four arms, four legs and two faces. They were so nearly perfect that they rivaled the gods who, acting out of envy and fear, cut the spheres into two halves, one feminine and one masculine. Ever since then, as the myth continues, the two severed parts of the original human being have been striving to reunite. And when one meets his other half, the pair is lost in an amazement of love and friendship and intimacy.[1] Without the help of divine revelation, which we can claim for the author of Genesis, poets and philosophers seemed to come to the notion of this androgynous nature of human beings by intuition more than anything else.

We should be cautioned, however, not to take this intuition lightly. This image of the male-female dynamic struggle for unity becomes one paradigm for understanding God's struggle to gather a people to himself. At times God is a lover in pursuit of his beloved (Song of Songs), and at times a faithful spouse anguishing over his wayward wife, Israel (Hosea). Even Jesus sees himself as a bridegroom of his people, while St. Paul sees in the married couple's relationship a sign of Christ's love for the church. The human longing and struggle for unity is often caught up in the struggle characterized by the tension between the male and female forces in life.

Carl Jung

No single person has helped more to unravel the nature of this struggle than the Swiss psychologist Carl G. Jung. He is the first scientist to observe the masculine and feminine components of human nature. Man is not only a sexual being, he is also a bisexual being, combining within himself the masculine and feminine principles. The same is true of the woman, who combines both the feminine and masculine principles within herself. According the Jung, the feminine component of a man's personality is called the *anima*, and the masculine component in the woman's personality is called the *animus*. As John A. Sanford, a Jungian analyst and Episcopal priest explains in his book *The Invisible Partners*:

> Jung did not just dream up his idea of the anima and the animus, nor did he allow his ideas to remain on the level of creative intuition. . . . Jung was a scientist, and the scope of his scientific investigation was the human psyche, hence his ideas are grounded on psychological facts. Empirical evidence for the anima and animus can be found wherever the psyche spontaneously expresses itself. The anima and animus appear in dreams, fairy tales, myths, the world's great literature, and, most of all, in the varying phenomena of human behavior. For the anima and the animus are the Invisible Partners in every human relationship, and in every person's search for individual wholeness. Jung called them archetypes, because the anima and animus are essential building blocks in the psychic structure of every man and woman. If something is archetypal, it is typical. Archtypes form the basis for instinctive, unlearned behavior patterns that are common to all mankind, and represent themselves in human consciousness in certain typical ways. For Jung, the concepts of anima/animus explain a wide variety of psychic facts and form a hypothesis that is confirmed over and over again by empirical evidence.[2]

For the sake of our discussion here, we will accept the position that "masculine" and "feminine" qualities are a result of true psychological dissimilarities and not entirely the result of socially assigned roles and conditioning. While many may argue in favor of the latter, since men and women can perform many of the same functions in life, this actually supports the notion that each person is a combination of male and female polarities. It is because of a man's feminine side that he can perform in ways traditionally assigned to women, and vice versa.[3] While this does not negate cultural influences, to be sure, it certainly says there is a real difference between "masculine" and "feminine." Jung's studies make this point.

Traits

What are these qualities or traits that make men and women different from each other? Beyond the obvious physical and sexual differences, there seems to be differences in psychological needs and drives. A classic analysis reflecting Jung's thought is as follows:

FEMININE TRAITS	MASCULINE TRAITS
Humility	Self-possessiveness
Obedience	Responsibility
Openness	Closure
Receptivity	Assertiveness
Trust	Truth and Risk
Forgiveness	Confrontation
Patience	Decisiveness
Long Suffering	Carry-through
Tenderness	Tough Love

In looking at these traits (strengths or virtues), it becomes clear that those identified as feminine all support the deep need in women for belonging. On the other hand, the masculine traits all support the deep need in men for autonomy. As we indicated in the last chapter, all people have human emotional needs for love, belonging, self-worth, and autonomy. But women most often pursue love and self-worth in the context of their desire to belong. Most men pursue love and self-worth in the context of their desire for autonomy.

For example, a woman often finds her sense of fulfillment in her relationships. Nurturing instincts are important to her approach to life. As long as she has a sense of being needed by her husband, her children, or others, she is satisfied. But when she senses she is not the source of their happiness or love, she fears she is nothing. This is why it is difficult for some mothers to let go of their children when they grow up. The danger here is that should she not integrate masculine traits into her personality, her quest for closeness and relationship can become an all-consuming, self-focused, full-time job. The end result would be an unhealthy dependence on others. She would be stuck with a helpless-woman image.

Similarly, a man often finds his sense of fulfillment in his accomplishments. If he is not achieving great things and is not seen as a hero or "self-made man," he is nothing. This is why men often become workaholics, married more to their jobs than to their wives. Since they have not integrated the feminine side of their personalities into their lives, they are often totally oblivious to the resentment their wives feel toward their jobs. Their quest for approval and acceptance become an all-consuming, self-focused, full-time job. The end result is an unhealthy independence from others. Such men are stuck with a macho-man image.

Two Journeys of Integration

There is a need for the integration of the masculine-feminine sides of our personalities as human beings. If this does not happen, the powerful need for belonging in women deteriorates into unhealthy dependence, and the powerful need for autonomy in men deteriorates into unhealthy independence. But this integration cannot happen in isolation from others. It requires a love relationship with others. In other words, it is not good for the man to be alone because, without a healthy love relationship with others, he cannot fully develop into his manliness. Without someone to help him develop his feminine side, he will remain a macho man, which is really a man of stunted growth.

To put this another way, if the man does not journey into the feminine, that is, develop his feminine traits, he cannot journey into the deeper masculine he was intended to be as a man. If he remains concerned only with his macho image (incomplete masculine), he is dealing only with images, not reality. He confuses his quest for such goals as power, sex, and wealth with his real strength as a man: his being a person of principle, acting out of values that generate life in others as persons. Men who do not make this journey remain unattractive as men and must play the role of "manliness." Those who make this journey are attractive as men because of their genuine manliness.

This journey of integration of the masculine and feminine begins during a person's childhood. Parents play a significant role in it. In fact, the degree of integration of the *animus* and *anima* in their own personalities will determine what kind of models for adult life they will offer their children. An overly dependent mother or overly independent father cannot help but be unhealthy models. Even when both parents are well integrated, however, they still have unique roles to play in their child's development. As Father Richard Rohr, O.F.M., has said: "A mother can give permission to her son to be a man, but it takes his father to show him how to be a man."[4] The converse is true for girls growing up. A father can give permission for his daughter to become a woman, but it takes a mother to show her how to be a woman. Both parents have much to contribute to the healthy psychological development of their children. For the boy, a mother nurtures his need for belonging as he reaches to develop and test his masculinity. For a girl, a father supports her need for autonomy as she reaches to develop and test her femininity.

As time goes by, parents' influence wanes in favor of the influence of others. The ensuing socializing process is critical to the integration process. Unfortunately, the pressures of society, often present within the family itself, can interfere in a detrimental way. Cultural patterns have limited many a young girl to an exaggerated role of the nurturer, while young boys have grown up with the mistaken notion that showing feelings of warmth or tenderness were somehow a violation of their manliness. How many women were teased when young for being tomboys? How many men were taught at the earliest age that "big boys don't cry?" In such ways, girls often got the message that "autonomy" was not an acceptable goal for them, while boys grew up believing that "belonging" would be seen as a sign of weakness for them. Have you ever heard of a "henpecked" wife or of a bride about to lose her freedom? We pity the poor spinster but not so the bachelor. The messages of society are clear. Each in its own way frustrates the integration process of the masculine and feminine sides of the human personality. Consequently, there are countless women today who are hopelessly dependent on others for survival, and countless men who are hopelessly convinced they are less than men if they admit any need for others in their lives. Both are destined to lives that are less than they were created to live.

The First Journey

But there comes a time in a person's psychological growth when there must be an opening of oneself to another person or group of persons in love. From this natural life experience, the integration process often, but not always, takes giant leaps forward, regardless of past influences. Under normal circumstances, this happens in the "falling-in-love" process. It is the woman who brings out the *anima*, the feminine side of her beloved. It is the man who brings out the *animus*, the masculine side of his sweetheart. It is in the intimacy of the love-relationship that the woman actually finds herself and the man finds himself. "When I am with him, I feel so much more complete." "When I am with her, I feel like I am a better man." This is true because, in a real sense, they are. The love between them brings out the less dominant side of their personalities. They feel more complete because they are more complete. The journey of integration is now getting somewhere.

As a husband loves his wife, he frees her to experience her autonomy as a person. He helps her believe in her goodness and dignity apart from her role as mother. His love frees her to exercise the more masculine virtues. She finds it acceptable to be assertive, self-possessed, and decisive. As the couple's love deepens over the years, the wife journeys, as it were, into the masculine. An integrated husband will welcome this "passage," as his wife will be better prepared to share with him the leadership role in the family. Decisions for the family can be shared by both and not rest on his shoulders alone. But at the same time he still cherishes the femininity of his wife and has no desire to compromise or lessen it. On the one hand, he is giving her permission to develop her masculine side, and then invests himself into her journey so she can enter into a deeper femininity and be a woman in the fullest sense.

By completing the journey to the deeper feminine, a very attractive feminine energy becomes evident in the woman. She does not lose her femininity as she exercises the more masculine virtues. Rather than being dependent on her husband in an unhealthy way, the wife also welcomes his need for her. Interdependence replaces both dependence and independence in the relationship. The woman becomes more secure in her femininity and closer to wholeness as a person. Rather than competitors in life, she and her husband truly share a common life together.

Because of his wife's love for him, a husband, for his part, is permitted to journey into the feminine. He can show such inner qualities as warmth and tenderness without being threatened by outside pressures. While he feels the need for autonomy, he discovers that experiencing belonging with his wife does not really threaten it at all. His wife's love for him draws out his tender and caring side. While he may still hear the warnings of his youth, he realizes with a true sense of relief that it is okay to share these more feminine nurturing virtues with his wife. Needless to say, she welcomes this too, as care for the children, let's say, is not her responsibility alone.

But, like her husband toward her, a wife cherishes the masculinity of her husband and invests herself into his journey so that his deeper masculinity can be openly expressed. A husband has no need to be independent from his wife to be fully a man. He realizes that in his love relationship with her he comes closer to completeness as a person. At the same time, a very masculine energy emerges that makes him a very attractive person. He compromises nothing of his masculinity as he exercises the more feminine virtues. His self-possessiveness is not threatened by showing humility, patience, or tenderness. If anything, they hold his more masculine qualities in bold relief. The first to benefit from this journey to the deeper masculine is his wife.

The Second Journey

This so-called "second journey" into the deeper feminine/ masculine is critical to a person's journey to "completeness." Actually, the journey is never really complete for us.

If anyone experienced it, it had to have been Jesus, the fully human man. Actually, it is healthy to feel "incomplete." This provides us with a constant reminder that there is room for our growth as persons. (Pitiful is the one who thinks he/she has it all together.) There will always be a tension between the masculine and feminine energies at work within us and between us. While we may sense moments of this "completeness" now, it will come with consistency only with the joys of heaven. So this struggle for us must continue until then.

If a man stops after his journey into the feminine, he may gain popularity with some, but he is bound to compromise his masculinity. The same is true for a woman. If she tries to enter a "man's" world as a man, some may welcome the challenge, but she will compromise her femininity. The unique gifts she has to bring will be lost. Men need to be men, and women need to be women. If the second journey to wholeness is not entered, it puts men and women into competitive rather than complementary positions with one another. The end result is conflict rather than unity. This does not mean that men do not belong in the home nor women in the marketplace. They do, but as men and women. The same can be said of women's place in the church. They have gifts to bring to the decision-making process that men simply cannot bring in the same way. While the role of women in the church is a "rights issue," it is even more so a "needs issue" for the church. We do not need women with men's views or men with women's views. We need people who can speak from the depth of their personhood as women and men.

This, by the way, is one reason why married couples as married couples need to have more of a voice in the church. A truly sacramental couple will bring the values of relationship to the church's decision-making process. Interdependence is a way of life for them. They are not defensive about their masculinity or femininity. They can live in both worlds with a sense of openness and self-confidence. In fact, Raymond G. Hunthausen, Archbishop of Seattle, made the following point in his pastoral letter on the sacrament of matrimony to his people in 1982:

> Married couples can no longer be overlooked or excluded from influencial leadership roles. For we can no longer afford to ignore the singular value of sacramental couples for the church's life and mission. . . . It is not enough to confine married couples to an advisory role in areas which seem appropriate within the present perspective of church leadership structures. If we simply continue operating within the given framework, the charisms of matrimony will not achieve the influence that they warrent.[5]

Celibate Integration

While we have been examining how integration of the masculine and feminine traits takes place in the marital relationship, clearly the most common and easily understood way for it to happen, it is not the only way for it to happen. Single persons are not, by that fact, condemned to a life of "incompleteness" as persons. The journey toward the deeper masculine and feminine is available to them. But they cannot make that journey alone. Such integration requires that each has significant relationships with others, both men and women. While this is not as easily demonstrated as in the case of the committed, exclusive relationship of husband and wife, it is still possible.

The priesthood, however, is a way of life that does call for a committed relationship between a priest and his people. While a priest's journey into the feminine and through it to the deeper masculine is going to be obviously different from a married man's journey, it does follow some strikingly similar patterns. Furthermore, considering the significance of priesthood to the life of the church, it becomes imperative that a priest makes these journeys. Celibacy, as a charism of relationship, is an important factor in this integration process. It serves as a catalyst to a depth of relationship a priest needs with his people for it to happen.

It is not only for his own sake that a priest must make these journeys, but also for the sake of his people. If he does not make them, his masculinity will be neutralized. Or, to use a more sexual term, he may as well be neutered. Considering the past training of many priests, beginning the first journey may be the toughest part. But it is possible. With the grace of celibacy, it can be made easier. After all, a celibate is a sign of relatedness, maybe not as obvious as a husband with his wife, but just as real.

Beginning the Journey

Father Richard Rohr, O.F.M., in the same presentation referred to earlier, observed with great sadness the number of priests he had met who seemed to lack real energy as men. Rather than being attractive spiritual leaders, they had little self-confidence and were very inward and selfish; rather than being oriented toward community, they were prone to self-pity. It was common for them to be distant or macho-oriented, to identify success with achievement, and to rely on their positions of power to reach their goals. Father Rohr explained this phenomenon as evidence that these men, for whatever reason, were not in touch with their feminine strengths at all. Consequently, while they would try to project the externals of masculinity, they could not grasp it from within. The tragedy here is that unless these men made that first journey into the feminine, there was no way they could ever begin the second journey into the deeper masculine. Something needed to happen to them.

It was just this type of priest who was often deeply moved by such experiences as Marriage Encounter. In a rather dramatic fashion, they encountered themselves and their *anima*, possibly for the first time. It was nothing short of a profound revelation. In witnessing the tenderness of the husbands and wives for each other, they got in touch with their own warmth and tenderness. The couples reinforced this by reflecting back to the priests the importance of their nurturing capacity. They experienced love from the people simply for being priests. They did nothing to earn it. For some, it was similar to a "falling-in-love" experience. They felt as if they were better men, more complete as persons. And they were. Their journey into the feminine, that is, their becoming aware of their *anima* for the first time or as never before, was opening a whole new world within themselves to enter and explore.

Through the matrimonied couples, these priests heard the faithful of the church call them to a love relationship with them. It was the grace of celibacy that freed many of these priests to accept that invitation. But it was both priests and people who were touched by that grace. While it may have been unconscious, the people knew they had a special relationship with "their" priest. They knew it was right to invite him into relationship with them.

But a priest can begin this journey in many other ways as well. He can never, however, begin it alone. He needs others to call him out of his "pretend" masculine world. It could well be that this happens in his staff relationships or with special friends with whom he feels comfortable enough to become vulnerable. But it must come from people who genuinely love their priest and want him to grow as a man for his sake and the sake of the church. After all, he is "their" priest. He was ordained for them. They have a right and responsibility to help him become the best priest he can be. If he is open to their love, the journey can begin.

Under most circumstances, people are eager to see their priests make this leg of the journey. This is because the feminine virtues that come with it are generally idealized and trusted in our church, even society, today. Who can argue with humility, trust, patience, or forgiveness? And who can deny that people want their priests to be loving? Intimacy and belonging are central to it. Affirmation is important too. That is all some people want from their priest — to be affirmed by them. These are all beautiful and necessary qualities for a priest to have. As a man, he needs to be able to express himself in these ways. But if he is not careful, he may succumb to the temptation to remain there, having traveled only part way to his full masculinity. He may become stranded on a feminine detour.

Entering the Masculine

Celibacy is a charism that urges a priest to live his relationship with his people as a man. This means he must not settle for less than being fully masculine. But again, it is his people who make this possible by the way they relate to him. While they give him permission to develop his feminine side, they must also walk that journey with him in such a way that they do not suppress his masculinity. If they are truly invested in their priest, they will free him to exercise the masculine virtues for them as well as the feminine. Some may fear this will be a return to the macho-image of masculinity. Not so. Confidence will replace fear, and substance a shallow image; self-worth will overcome self-pity; and above all, an attractive masculine energy will replace a weak, unattractive male façade.

A priest's people, then, have a significant role to play in

his journey toward the deeper masculine. The charism of celibacy calls them to this. But how they treat their priest will betray the investment they are willing to make. On the one hand, a priest told how he had received two dolls as gifts from parishioners. One was a cute little ceramic figurine, the other was an Infant of Prague with a complete change of clothing. Obviously, the ladies' intentions were good, but what were these gifts saying? It is hard to imagine them giving dolls to their husbands. Some people would be happy to see their priests journey into the feminine and stay there. On the other hand, another priest relates how he was challenged by some close friends to be more courageous in his preaching. He had told them how he held back opinions that might upset his people because they went against the mainstream. Rather than preach the Gospel he felt in his heart, he gave them a bland substitute. One of his friends said, "We need you to be a prophet for us. We need you to risk your comfort for us and the sake of the Gospel. We will still love you." That priest will never hear a clearer call to journey into the deeper masculine. He accepted it because he knew he would not travel that journey alone. People of faith had invested themselves to travel with him. Without them, he may well have continued to compromise his masculinity. Instead, he soon afterward asked for a parish assignment to a poor, racially tense area of Los Angeles.

Unlike the feminine virtues, the masculine virtues are not readily trusted or idealized in our church or society today. No one likes to rock the boat. Rather than be decisive, the message is "be patient." Rather than speak the truth to call people to responsibility, we are told to remain open and not judge. Rather than love as a man, which can be challenging and tough, we are expected only to love as a woman, with tenderness and warmth. Rather than confront those who hurt us, we are supposed to exercise long suffering. Rather than challenge our people to accountability, they tell us they would rather we affirm them. Father Rohr tells of a community he had affirmed for ten years, but nothing ever happened to them. If anything, they became only more inward. As he put it, "How many times can you redecorate the rec room?" That community did not need affirmation; it needed confrontation; it needed to be challenged.

The point here is that only when priests journey through the feminine into the deeper masculine can their full energy as men appear. It is only then that they will be truly attractive as men of the church, capable of providing the spiritual leadership that the church needs from them as men. The charism of celibacy facilitates this process. It helps a priest love his people as a man. At the same time, it helps his people see his attractiveness as a man. Because of the love relationship between a priest and his people, he can confront them when they need to be confronted, make hard decisions for their good, and still be trusted. He is free to risk, even to fail, and still be a man.

This is simply saying that there are times when feminine virtues are inappropriate to the situation, and masculine virtues are called for. There are times when a priest must preach the tough messages of the Gospel, messages the people may not want to hear. Teaching the dangers of wealth to the wealthy should not be skipped over, nor the challenges of the social Gospel to all our people. In our efforts to be sensitive and nonjudgmental of others, we seldom hear the word "sin" from the pulpit anymore. Maybe it is time we speak the truth about sin as we see it, even if it makes some people feel guilty. After all, if they do not experience guilt, the call to repentance will ring pretty hollow.

Our vocation as teachers of the Word is to be faithful to that Word. It is not always pleasant news. If all we preach is the "soft" Gospel, what the people want to hear, we have turned Jesus into a "soft" Jesus who died, not for our sins, but so that we could feel good! To the extent we do this, we neuter Jesus and neutralize his Gospel. Rather than a call to a whole new way of life, it becomes a spineless rubber stamp of the "nice" life most of us live. Jesus, the man, moved between the feminine and masculine continually in his ministry. He was every bit as stern and challenging as he was warm and tender. There is a tremendous need for priests today to reflect the masculinity of Jesus in their lives. This is one aspect of the *alter Christus* that they can take aim at.

Celibate Energy

Rather than a celibate being something other than a man, there is one thing a priest clearly needs to be: a man. He should be one who witnesses energy within himself, and that energy is both masculine and feminine. Celibacy serves this end. It frees a priest to be that man his people need at any given time. This is not to be confused with "being all things to all men." A priest still carries within himself his limitations as a man in need of nurturing and challenging, just like his people. Rather, it means he is free to be with his people as they need him to be.

Celibacy leads to a way of being, not of functioning. A priest's attractiveness does not come from some title he holds, role he fills, or vestment he wears. In fact, should such things become too important to him, he should be a concern to his people. Nor does it come from his successes as a pastor or his ability to do everything right. His attractiveness comes from his ability to be life-giving to his people. When they are around him, they feel better about themselves or see their own need to grow. His attractiveness comes from the level of integration of the masculine and feminine sides of his personality, from his approaching the "complete" man.

His attractiveness elicits a special fondness and trust from married men and women. They sense that he adds something to their relationship because of his celibate love for them. They trust him in ways not normally open to married men or to bachelors. In many ways, they are accepted as part of the family. Open signs of love and affection are not seen as odd or inappropriate. Parents are even willing to entrust their children to his care. Many are thrilled to see their children having a special relationship with their priest. In a negative sort of way, I suppose this is why the scandal is so great when a celibate priest takes advantage of the unique relationship he has with his people. He has violated not only their trust but also their faith.

One of the great gifts a celibate priest has to offer the church is his vision. While he knows the church must exercise the nurturing virtues of caring for the poor, healing the broken, and reconciling the separated, he cannot help but keep an eye toward the future and where the events of today are leading. It is a matter of the old pioneers vs. pilgrims story. While a priest in parish work needs the more feminine, settler virtues to keep his parish going, he cannot lose sight of the fact that he is the leader of a pilgrim church. His masculine virtues are equally needed. Psychologically and spiritually, the church is a people on the move. From this awareness comes his sense of mission to the community, diocese, and even the world. So important is this vision that if a priest sees the condition of the larger world as irrelevant to his parochial world, he may well be the one who has become irrelevant.

It is a priest's vision that will keep urging his people to growth as well. If our young have no sense of excitement about serving the church as priests or religious, it may be because we have not been seen as people of vision by them. If our married couples are not aware of their dignity as living sacraments of the church, it may be because they have never heard it. While we must help our hurting families, we also have a responsibility every bit as urgent to help our married couples know just how important they are to the renewal and life of the church. Only then can we be about empowering them to fulfill their mission to their brothers and sisters in faith. Whether or not they accept the challenge is not in our control, but that they hear the challenge is. That is the kind of vision we need to share.

For example, a husband and wife, as a sacrament for the church, struggle to integrate their masculine and feminine qualities so they can be "one body," not just for their own sakes but also for the sake of the church. Their "oneness" offers a sign of hope to the church that it too can integrate its masculine and feminine qualities so that it "may be one." But this unity is not just for the church's sake. It is also for the sake of the world. Only to the degree that this masculine/feminine integration happens within the church can it be a clear sacrament of Christ to the world. In other words, just as a male- or female-dominated marriage is a poor sacramental sign, so too is a male- or female-dominated church a poor sacramental sign.

There are, then, three levels at which this integration must take place in the church: within the individual person, especially the celibate priest as a community leader; within the institution of sacramental marriage, as a sign of loving relationship to which the Christian community is called; and within the church itself, among its membership with one another, so it can be a sacrament of Christ to the world. No one else in the church today seems to have the opportunity or influence to articulate this vision with credibility as does the celibate priest. This might be because no one sees things quite the way he does.

In the eyes of many in the world, a celibate priest may appear to be less than a man. He is not upwardly mobile. His interests are not money, sex, or getting ahead. He is even willing to look foolish for the things he believes in. His goal in life is simply to be a man for his people, living out of his strengths as one who does not shy away from the feminine within him or compromise the masculine about him. Celibacy is the divine gift that helps all this to happen. God knows no man could do it by himself.

In many ways, the meaning of a celibate priest's life defies description. His manhood has little to do with sweat, brawn, or power. There are moments when it is empty and moments when it is full, just like any man's life. But it is a man's life. As a celibate man, he has more than a statement to make; poetically speaking, he has a song to sing. He wants to share with his people not just his talents, insights, or good deeds. He wants them to sing the song of life too! He wants his people to become caught up in the Spirit of God, the ultimate source of his sexuality. He longs to make the words of Jesus his own, "Love one another as I have loved you."

5

Contract or Covenant?

When a man reflects on his vocation to the priesthood, he is conscious of two things: that the call is from God and that it must come through the people of the church. He is not looking for a job but for a life of involvement with the community of faith, a life that holds out the opportunity for fulfillment and satisfaction. Otherwise he would not accept the call. He knows there is no such thing as a self-appointed priest. So if the vocation from God is not somehow verified by the people of the church through the official call of a bishop, he realizes he cannot be ordained to the sacrament of Orders. Even when a person believes he has a genuine call from God to the ordained priesthood, he knows he cannot be admitted to Orders unless that call also comes from the believing community. The bishop certifies that call. It should also be noted that if a bishop were to ordain someone to the priesthood without reference to the church, that ordination would be suspect.

Living beyond Justice

The significance of the faithful in the life of a priest is not to be taken lightly, either before or after ordination. But the underlying issue is the nature of that relationship itself. Is it a contract or a covenant? If it is fundamentally a contract that the priest enters into with the people of the church, then their relationship will be based on justice. Priesthood will be seen as the fulfilling of duties, a living up to a job description agreed upon between priest and people. But if it is fundamentally a convenant, then the priest and people will see their relationship as a free offering of one to the other. Love, which is a step beyond justice, will be central to their relationship. Rather than evaluating the relationship solely in terms of what they do for one another, the standard for evaluation will be who they are with one another. While the contractual relationship may be easier to understand and measure, it is the covenant relationship that reflects the primary values of the Gospel.

It is clear from New Testament thought that matrimony is meant to be a clear sign of the covenant relationship. The relationship between a husband and wife is a sacramental sign of the love relationship Jesus has with his church. Since Jesus commanded his followers to "Love one another as I have loved you" (John 15:12), it is evident he wanted the church itself to be a model of the covenant relationship. If this were not true, the church could not be a sacrament of his love for the world. Consequently, it would be totally out of character for Jesus to expect his priests to settle for anything less than a covenant relationship with their people.

In accepting the sacrament of orders, a man chooses to enter a committed relationship with those people who, under the influence of the Holy Spirit, have invited him to be their priest. He expresses his response not by just saying "I am here to serve you," but by using the words of Jesus as his own, "I am *in your midst* as one who serves you" (Luke 22:28). He has committed himself to belong to them, not just to minister to them. Yet the attitude he has toward his people is even more intimate than that. Drawing again on the Spirit of Jesus, the priest must be prepared to say sooner or later, "I call you friends" (John 15:15). He knows Jesus had identified the disciples as "friends" because he had made known to them everything from his Father. He had shared himself and his own intimacy with his Father with his disciples. This should express the desire of the priest's heart toward his people as well. After all, Jesus did not say, "Serve one another as I have served you," but "Love one another as I have loved you."

A priest also hears the words of St. Paul applying to his relationship with his people, "Defer to one another out of reverence for Christ" (Eph. 5:21). His desire is to treat them with deference, not indifference. He is not only ready to love his people, he is equally open to receive their love in return. It is as if the church had proposed to him, and he has responded by choosing to give himself totally to them in return. He was asked to lead them, and he does so by inviting them to live their dignity with him as the People of God, the Bride of Christ.

There is a beautiful liturgical expression of this reality when the priest enters the church to celebrate Mass. He comes from the people in procession to the altar to lead them in worship, and then returns to them when the celebration is completed. He does not ascend the altar on his own, but does so because he has been called to do so by his people. Nor does he leave the altar to be about his own business. He literally returns to those people with whom he is expected to share his journey of faith.

Significance of the Bishop

While this depth of relationship may not be explicitly stated when a priest is assigned to a parish, it is implied by the fact that his bishop is the one who assigned him there. The priest is actually sharing in the priesthood of his bishop who has a most explicit relationship with the people of his diocese.

Should a priest change dioceses or join a diocese for which he was not ordained, he must be incardinated, which is an official declaration of his belonging to the bishop and people of the diocese. It is as though the church is guarding herself against having any "free-lance" priests. This is not just a matter of church law but rather the very nature of priesthood, which requires this explicit relationship of a priest with the people of the church. For this reason, his priestly activity is approved by his bishop one way or the other. What this is saying is that the significance of the faithful to the life of a priest cannot be forgotten. In terms of his priestly dealing with them, they are not meant to be his clients but his people, to whom he is committed by a covenant of love.

An Arranged "Marriage"

There is one major flaw in this appealing scenario. In practice, the people have very little to say about who will be their priests. The process by which men are called to the priesthood has become so formalized that the voice of the people is almost an incidental formality. In most cases, if a man wants to be a priest, he can be, as long as he is capable of being properly trained and is judged to be morally and psychologically sound. The issue of his desire to belong to his people, to love and be loved by them, is often lost in the process. Furthermore, the people are expected to take whomever they are sent. In some ways, it is like the dying practice of an arranged marriage.

Marriages used to be arranged, often for economic or social reasons, by a couple's parents, usually their fathers. Little if any attention was paid to whether or not the couple loved each other. As long as the man could function as a husband and provide for his family, that is all that mattered.

Unhappily, the attitude behind this dying practice still

finds life in the church. When priestly training concentrates on how well a man can function as a priest and provide for his people, even if it be done unconsciously, the same message is being sent: "The relationship you have with one another is secondary."

This is not to deny the need for priests to be well trained in theology or to have the necessary competencies to fulfill their priestly duties. There is no substitute for them today, but they are not everything. It is just not enough if a priest is expected to live a personally fulfilling life, which requires his living a committed love-relationship with his people. If love is not central to his life, both he and his people will sense something is missing.

This awareness was expressed beautifully and simply in the stage play *Fiddler on the Roof*. After seeing two of his daughters marry for love, and not as he and his wife had married, as an arrangement in keeping with the tradition of their time and culture, Tevye begins to wonder about his relationship with Golde, his wife of twenty-five years. So he asks her, "Do you love me?" After her initial objection to the question as foolish, she finally answers as though she had discovered something new, "I guess I do!" The song ends with both singing together, "It is good to know." It is not foolish for a priest to wonder about the place of love in his life. It is good for him to know he is loved by his people and for them to know that they are loved by him. There must be some way to underscore the importance of this love-relationship.

The People's Choice

It is here that celibacy again enters the scenario. When celibacy is understood and lived, there is no way to take the love relationship between a priest and his people lightly. Unfortunately, however, like the call to priesthood itself, there is no explicit evidence of a call from the people to the priest expressing their desire for him to live a celibate way of life for them. Worse still, they view celibacy as something that does not involve them at all. It is something mysterious their priest must live by himself. The faithful have no notion that they are indispensable to his celibate way of life, that he cannot live it without them. Rather than a church decision, celibacy is viewed as a decision the priest makes all alone, or one that the institutional church makes for him, to which he succumbs.

In our society today, we would not let a man choose a wife without her willingness to be his wife. It would not matter how altruistic he may be in choosing her, even if he sincerely believes it is for her sake. It is up to her to accept or reject his invitation to marry. She has no obligation to just sit still and take it. The same is true for celibacy. The faithful have to decide whether they want to extend their charism to a particular man. Celibacy should not be his private choice irrespective of them. In fact, the faithful should have much to say about how he lives out his acceptance of their invitation. Fidelity to the vow of celibacy will not be something he owes primarily to the institutional church but to the people of the church, to those who asked him to be celibate for them. If this is not the case, the people are put in the position of being takers. At best they will be cheerful observers of their priest, standing on the sidelines of his life. They will not become involved with him because they were never invited to in the first place. While they may even be happy and very well pleased because their priest is such a good man, they will feel no real urgency to share in his life. In fact, they have little to say about how he lives his life, as long as it is not openly "sinful."

This is a sad situation. Most people are not conscious of their importance to their priests, because the whole concept of celibacy never included their role in it. As noted above, this situation would not be tolerated in our society today in the case of the woman who had to accept marriage against her personal preference. Even if her husband cared for her well, she would know her place: Her opinions about the marriage would be considered unimportant and her part in her husband's life would be determined only by him. Their relationship would not only be terribly deficient, it would also be terribly degrading to the woman. The man's sense of superiority would be dreadful, cutting off all possibility for a healthy relationship. The best that could happen is that they would function well together. Unfortunately, this is what has happened in the church. By and large, its priests are extraordinarily good men, especially generous in their service to their people. But many have missed their celibacy altogether. It is simply not an expression of their relationship with their people, either on their part or their people's.

A Shared Responsibility

Catholics on the average simply have no sense of a personal responsibility for the celibacy of their priests, other than to encourage them to stick it out. Personal love has nothing to do with it. Nor are Catholics on the average aware that their priest's celibacy is a statement of who they are to him — that they are central to his life. They have no notion that celibacy means the priest is willing to be accountable to them. So poorly is this understood that for the most part Catholics do not believe they can or should make any kind of suggestion to their priest in personal terms of their expectations of how he lives the charism of celibacy for them. This usually translates into an attitude that the priest is not their concern. But since celibacy is so closely linked to how a priest lives his priesthood, many think that is not their concern either.

Celibacy is not just for the sake of the priest or his people. It is for their relationship together, which is for the sake of the church. This is too important to allow the current situation of uninvolvement to continue. But it will unless the faithful recognize their rightful place in a priest's call and his living out of celibacy. They must realize that the priestly vocation, whether celibate or married, is not one that comes directly from God but through them.

This is not a new idea. It is totally consistent with God's way of acting throughout the history of salvation. He works through people. The church reawakened to this reality in its recent revisions of the rites for baptism and confirmation. In the *Rite of Christian Initiation of Adults*, the importance of the faithful in the formation of the catechumens has been clearly and emphatically stated:

> The initiation of catechumens takes place step by step in the midst of the community of the faithful. Together with the catechumens, the faithful reflect upon the value of the paschal mystery, renew their own conversion, and by their example lead the catechumens to obey the Holy Spirit more generously. (no. 4)

The preparing of converts to the church is of such great importance that it cannot be left to the private domain of the priest by himself. Besides information, the candidates are in need of formation in the faith. This requires involvement with the faithful. Once received in the church, the process that has begun continues. The people continue to form the neophytes. While they were called by God to the church, the people's reinforcement of that call makes it a life-giving experience for them.

This same sort of thing should be recognized in the calling of candidates to the priesthood. They must be formed into being priests of the people. This process cannot be left only to the structures of the institutional church. The faithful merit direct involvement. Somehow priests must sense being called forth by the faithful for the faithful. Anything that encourages the notion that priesthood is something between God and the candidate alone, without explicitly including the people, must end. Those who have provided the environment that opens someone to the vocation of priesthood deserve a real place in the process of their selection.

Somehow the faithful must be helped to see a priest as "their man," not just "God's man." Better yet, they should come to see their priest as God's man only because he belongs to God's people. Furthermore, both people and priest need to realize a man in orders lives out his vocation not just by doing good things for his people but by responding to the call he received from them to be their lover. If this does not happen, priests will continue to be seen as somehow suspended between God and their people, rather than as living in their midst, journeying with them, sharing the pain of common sorrows, and enjoying the fruits of mutual love. If this were not so, "living in the Spirit" would just be empty words.

As a charism of relationship, both parties to celibacy must be involved in its being lived out in the church. A priest cannot choose to be celibate without involving the faithful any more than a man can choose to be married without involving the woman. Unless she says "yes" somewhere along the way, he is doomed to either a life of fantasy or frustration. In some way, therefore, the faithful need to call their priests to a celibate way of life, and the priest needs some way to respond openly. If this has not been done before ordination, it must be done afterward. Only when priests know that their celibacy is actually valued by their people can they ever begin to develop a positive and life-giving attitude toward it.

A Surprise Witness

A priest once said he was ordained fifteen years before anyone ever thanked him for being a celibate. The thanks came from a married couple. In fact, they thanked him for being a celibate *for* them. He was so surprised he could not respond. He had never heard anything like that before. He did not even know he was supposed to be living his celibacy for them. From all his previous experience he would never have guessed that anyone even cared. Celibacy had always been such a private thing. He had thought of it only in terms of what it was doing to him, the difficulties he experienced from the separate life style he was living, how generous he had appeared to his people, how free he was to serve them. He thought that he alone, by himself, was the witness to celibacy. He could choose to be its hero or its martyr. The perceived value of celibacy was in his control.

This priest may have been a witness to integrity, perseverance, and even heroism, but by himself he could not be a witness to celibacy. In reality, his life may not even have been a witness to the Gospel. The message of the Gospel is relationship. Jesus is revealed through the community of believers. Personal integrity is expected of all human beings as part of their response for their very existence. That is the vocation of creation. Celibates are not, by that fact, any more heroic than the married, dedicated singles, religious, or widowed. On the contrary, if celibacy calls attention just to the priest, he has missed the whole point of this charism. Even if it is personally satisfying and very good for some priests, they are supposed to be men of the church, not just their own men. This does not mean primarily men of the institutional church but men of the faithful. The people of the church have a right to know just how beautiful and attractive they are that their priest has chosen to give himself to them above all others or an other.

Celibate Fidelity

Again, the sacrament of matrimony can guide us here. No matter how faithful a husband may be in the sense of not engaging in sex with a woman other than his wife, that is not what marital fidelity is about. He has to be faithful by being a lover to the woman who is his wife. Fidelity is a positive virtue, not a privation. The prime motive behind a husband's fidelity to his marriage vows is not his dedication to his personal responsibility but his being absorbed in his wife. That alone is worthwhile. Any involvement with another woman is simply unthinkable because his mind, heart, and soul are so filled with his beloved. Similarly, he does not see his life with her as a matter of fulfilling duties. That makes marriage a contract. Rather, he is so conscious of her throughout his waking day that he cannot help but be responsive to her. In other words, what keeps him faithful is not his determination to do good and avoid evil; it is his positive attitude toward his wife. He is so filled with her that there is simply no room for anyone else. Such a husband does not have to be told that avoiding infidelity is not the same as fidelity. He knows fidelity in marriage concerns itself primarily with how much he and his wife enjoy each other, not with their success in avoiding sexual contact "outside the marriage." The focus of fidelity is their covenant love relationship, not a lack of illicit activity with someone else.

Celibacy is a charism of the church, for the church, and with the church, the whole People of God. It is not a private affair of the priest. Therefore, fidelity for the celibate is not the avoidance of sex but a positive affirmation of the people for whom he was ordained. It is not an expression of dedicated heroism but a shout of delight in his people. It is not the fulfilling of duties but the celibate's response to those people who are so special that he cannot leave them alone.

Celibacy should really be a testimonial to how a priest's people are so great, wonderful, and attractive that they could actually call him to a celibate way of life, and that he could look at that as a favor rather than a sacrifice. They should experience a love from their priest that says there is simply no room for anyone else.

A Matter of Attitude

This is a matter of attitude. It is most obvious in the newly ordained, though not exclusively, since they project a genuine enthusiasm for their people. They want to be with them, spend themselves for them, be one with them. This zeal gives rise to two dangers that such priests have to face. The first is burnout. Should they translate their priesthood solely into a ministry of service where they give, give, give, sooner or later they will find themselves disillusioned and empty because they did not realize they had a profound need to receive back from their people. The people, of course, had no idea they had a responsibility to give themselves to their priest in return, especially on a personal basis. The second danger are older priests who kid the young ones about being too enthusiastic. The message is clear: "The oils are still wet on your hands, but you will get over it." It is very much like the married men who remind the bridegroom, "The honeymoon won't last forever." In both instances expectations are lowered. After all, who wants to be pegged as "immature"? And if the priest is still enthusiastic after several years, the poor fellow is simply pegged as "too idealistic."

One rather enthusiastic older priest, however, shared the following story. While flying across the country, he struck up a conversation with the passenger next to him, a professed Mormon. It was not long before the issue of celibacy surfaced. Aware of Mormon attitudes about marriage(s), the priest chose not to talk about the popular notions of celibacy, being unmarried and living alone. He decided, instead, to describe the people of his parish as his spouse and how important they were to him. If anyone could handle the notion of having a relationship with many people, he figured his Mormon friend could. Not only was the priest free of defensiveness, he projected a genuine enthusiasm for what he was saying. His people did mean a lot to him, which his rather surprised traveling partner could tell. Furthermore, the priest projected a sense of optimism about the priesthood that is often lost when discussions turn to celibacy. The charism of celibacy supported and highlighted the significance of the priest's being a bridegroom to his spouse, the church. By the time they landed, the Mormon had no doubts about what the charism of celibacy meant as far as that priest was concerned: a gift from God meant to enhance the mutual relationship between himself and his people. He may have questioned the theory behind what the priest said, but he could not argue with the priest's enthusiasm.

The theory of celibacy is pointless until it is lived. As a charism of relationship, it requires more than an enthusiastic priest. The implication of this for the faithful is clear: They have to acknowledge their role in lived celibacy. They cannot be indifferent to it. Celibacy does not exist in the abstract. Only celibates exist and only in the here-and-now relationships they have with their people.

While celibates cannot belong to all the people of the church in the same way, they can live their celibacy for the sake of all the faithful by being lovingly responsive to the people to whom they are called to belong in a unique and special way from day to day. Those people must be lovingly responsive as well. They cannot view celibacy as something disembodied from those men who have chosen to live their lives for them. Even if some do not believe that celibacy is a good idea, they cannot allow their priests to carry it as a burden all by themselves. That would be infidelity to their priests. By assuming their part in the covenant relationship, they can help to ease the burden if one is there and positively transform it into an experience of joy. Celibacy should not be a burden. It is a grace from God offered through the faithful to their priests for deepening their mutual love.

A Fatal Flaw

From what has been said, it becomes clear that celibacy cannot survive as long as it is viewed simply as a restrictive law in the church or as something a priest is to live in isolation from his people. Contrary to current thought, it is not meant to be a contractual agreement forbidding marriage that a priest signs with the church before his ordination. Nor is it meant to be an agreement to live without sex that he makes to a cold institution. Celibacy is a charism of the Spirit that invites a priest to enter into a covenant relationship with the Body of Christ. Unfortunately, this is not what most men had in mind the day they committed themselves to a life of celibacy, so strong was the emphasis on what they were giving up. But even if it were, few of the faithful had any inkling of being a party to such a covenant with their priests. By default, priests were and are sentenced to live celibacy alone. In this we find the fatal flaw in celibacy as it is being lived today. It will no more work than a marriage will when only one party is committed to the marital covenant. The nature of celibacy, like the nature of marriage, requires mutuality of commitment to the covenant.

Because celibacy is treated like a contract a priest makes with the institutional church, he is not seen as a celibate by his people at all. He is seen as a man without a wife. Since adults are hesitant to allude to this, it takes children in their innocence to bring it up. "Do you have children?" they ask their pastor who is over for dinner. Nervously, their parents try to answer with, "Oh no, he's a priest. He is not married." Oops! It's out! Priests themselves, however, do not do much better. When asked, "Do you have a wife?" how often they answered, "My breviary is my wife." Not only is the answer unintelligible, it is also a nonanswer.

Not only is a priest seen as a man without a wife, he is also seen by many as a bachelor. He lives alone and appears to be lonely. Nothing about his life style is any more attractive than the way a lot of single men live. At least they have the option of getting married if they want to and can change jobs if they go stale. And we wonder why parents do not pray for their sons to be priests! (A parallel exists for religious sisters.) The priesthood is not attractive to many because their perception of the way a priest is supposed to live is not attractive.

But before we judge too quickly on this, we have to ask why the bachelor life style is so attractive to some priests. Can we lay the blame at their feet only? Might it not be because they are tired of trying to love someone who does not love them back? Is it because no one ever said "Thank you" to them for being celibate as if they really cared? Could it not be because they became so discouraged hearing people talk about celibacy as the waste of a good man? After a while the only defense is to get away from such talk. Even though many priests have opted for a bachelor way of life, it would be tragic if they were now judged as lacking sincerity or dedication to the church. They are good men and want to do a good job for their people. They are just like so many married people who, for one reason or the other, have settled for less than their dreams.

The People's Right to Know

Celibacy is something our people need to understand not only for their priest's sake but also for theirs. If they do not realize they are a critical factor in the celibate equation, the purpose of this charism will be forever frustrated. They cannot take responsibility for their part in the celibate relationship if they are unaware of having any responsibility in the first place. As long as this situation lasts, celibacy will never be something the average Catholic (lay or priest) can be proud of or take delight in. There will continue to be those embarrassing moments when someone, not knowing better, brings it up. There will be difficulty finding any visible differences between somebody celibate and somebody not. Priests will continue to evaluate celibacy by asking, "Am I keeping it?" The real question, "Are my people rejoicing in my celibacy?" will never cross their minds. It will never be a gift from and for the faithful but a burden to be borne or freed of.

It is a mistake to treat celibacy as a way of life the priest has chosen for himself or as a restriction imposed upon him by the institutional church, which he neither likes nor can do anything about. Celibacy must become a church decision. It needs to be treated as an invitation from the community of believers as a way they desire their priests to relate to them. A priest needs to realize he is being asked to be a celibate rather than just practice celibacy. He needs to know it is not just to preserve the institution of the church but to build up the believing community in love as the continuing incarnation of the Body of Christ.

6

Fellowship or Communion?

As soon as we say the church is the Body of Christ, we are talking about a living reality. It is not primarily an organization, company, or business. It is the People of God living in a relationship of love with one another. If the relationship were based on a contract between the people of the church, each person could say, "I will love you if . . . " or "I will love you because . . . " But as soon as we acknowledge that the relationship is a covenant between the people, each must say, "I will love you in spite of . . . " There are no conditions on this covenant. There is no writing anyone off. We must share the vision of St. Paul when he said, "Owe no debt to anyone except the debt that binds us to love one another" (Rom. 13:8).

Whenever the church is viewed as a business operation, someone surfaces as the boss, not as leader. Unfortunately, priests are often thrust into this role, one they too often find seductively attractive. They are seen to have power over their people, who thereby become their subjects. And since the bottom line of power is control, it is not surprising that someone gets hurt when conflicts arise. But priests are not meant to be bosses of anyone. They are meant to be leaders, even great leaders. The key is love, not power. As Jesus said at the Last Supper, "Earthly kings lord it over their people. . . . Yet it cannot be that way with you. Let the greater among you be as the junior, the leader as the servant" (Luke 22:25–26). When conflict occurs, there is no place for domination of anyone, because the bottom line of love is forgiveness and reconciliation.

This contrast is lived out in countless homes. When one member of a family believes he has power over the others, someone eventually gets hurt. A husband who thinks he has power over his wife may even be tempted to abuse her physically. Should a wife seek control over her husband, she will look for ways to abuse him. Somewhere along the way their covenant love reverted to a contract of duties they owed to each other. The focus narrowed to self. But in those homes where covenant love is strong, the focus remains on the other. When conflicts occur, attention is given to healing the relationship, not to winning the fight. A loving husband and wife seek forgiveness and reconciliation not just seven times, but "seventy times seven times" (Matt. 18:22). This is the way of life for those in a covenant relationship.

A Way of Loving for Life

The most essential thing about celibacy is that it is a way of loving for life. Rather than giving up, it is a taking on of the development of all those qualities of a real love relationship that should evidence a covenant of love: affection, tenderness, passion, desire; patience, closeness, listening, surrender—not to forget a readiness to confront and challenge when love demands it. Unfortunately, the word "love" is a misunderstood word. Most people either equate it with romantic feelings or sexual attraction. This is very inadequate even in the man-woman marital relationship, since feelings come and go or can be experienced toward other people even in the best of marriages. Such feelings do not require any real relationship at all. This does not say that the qualities of sensitivity, warmth, openness, and mutual respect that intimacy makes possible are not colored by our sexual nature. But in its most basic sense, intimacy is not the same as genital sexuality, although it does involve that for two persons joined together in covenant marriage.

Nor is love, as we are using it here, to be equated with acts of charity. For example, to take an unconscious person who has collapsed on the street to the hospital is certainly a good deed, an act of benevolent love, but it does not require intimate love. It can be done out of a sense of duty or of feeling sorry, because there is no one else to help the victim. For this act to be truly one of love of intimacy, there must be a relationship of some kind between the two persons.

For a relationship to be meaningful, each party must have knowledge of the other as a person. Not only must one listen to the other to discover who he is, there must be a willingness to reveal oneself in return. As Cardinal Joseph Bernardin of Chicago notes, "Intimacy involves . . . the willingness to disclose oneself to others, to become somewhat vulnerable by being honest about oneself . . . and a willingness to let others become a part of and an influence on one's own life."[1] Commenting on this, Father Don Conroy, director of the National Institute on the Family, says, "Intimacy in this sense obviously involves risk. As the spiritual writers tell us, an encounter with God or with a fellow human being is dangerous, for often it demands radical change in us. But the rewards of authentic Christian intimacy are worth the risks. The prime model of this kind of intimacy is, of course, Jesus."[2]

Revealing Oneself

The quality of the celibate relationship a priest has with his people is therefore contingent upon how well they know one another. The priest needs to let his people know who he is, his blood family, his likes and dislikes and history. Part of that history is his relationships with his bishop and brother priests. The people even need to know about his relationship with Jesus Christ and the Father and how open he is to be guided by the Spirit. They should be aware of his prayer life, hopes and dreams, hurts and fears. While this sounds like an invasion of privacy, it is no more than is expected between a husband and wife. In accepting the sacrament of Orders, like the sacrament of matrimony, a man chooses a life of relationship, not privacy.

In return, the priest needs to know who his people are as people, not just their needs as clients. What are their hopes, dreams, and fears? Who is God to them? What are the deepest longings of their hearts? There just seems to be no other way for a priest to apply to himself the words of Jesus, the Good Shepherd, "I know my sheep and my sheep know me in the same way that the Father knows me and I know the Father; for these sheep I give my life" (John 10:14–15). Jesus places no conditions on his self-giving, even if it means giving up his life. This is the meaning of passionate love. It is totally other-centered. There is no way around it, a priest who wants to live a celibate way of life has to be willing to give up his privacy.

The point of all this is not just to help the priest and people be more responsive to one another, or to elicit more mutual support, or to understand the other's feelings better. That is just looking at things from a human point of view. While this may be good as far as it goes, it may also be self-serving. The real issue is how willing a priest and his people are to be vulnerable to one another, to place themselves in the hands of the other, to be formed and shaped by the other. Are they willing to accept priesthood as a call to a love relationship or to settle for its being only a ministry? Considering the nature of celibacy, it becomes increasingly evident that the more it is reverenced and understood, the more priesthood will be reverenced and understood as well.

The Need to Risk

This means that a priest must be willing to put himself in a position to live in a full-fledged relationship with his people, to be known as a person and to know them as persons. It will require enough confidence in the goodness of his people to risk their rejection. This is not an invitation to irresponsibility, like sharing confessional matter or developing an exclusive relationship with someone. Nor does it require a priest to share indiscriminately his inner thoughts and fears with people who can use them against him. It is an invitation to break out of that protective shell that keeps people from recognizing he is a genuine human being with feelings and hopes. Parishioners deserve to know their priest is not perfect but one who is in the process of growth, just like they are.

While there is no blueprint to offer in this regard, ways must be found to encourage these values. For instance, any depth of relationship between priest and people is hardly possible when personnel policies of most dioceses remove priests from parishes on a routine basis. If a priest knows he will not be in a parish any length of time, he will be less apt to open himself to his people. It will make the inevitable separation too painful. The same can be said on behalf of the people. Why invest much with the priest if he is to be leaving soon? It is understandable why there is an actual grieving process that priest and people go through at such times. One priest was transferred from the parish he had founded almost twenty years earlier and actually went into a deep depression not unlike that experienced by a person going through the wrenching experience of divorce. Another priest, who is a pastor in a distant part of his diocese, commented as follows when asked if he wanted to transfer after a few years: "I am in no hurry. After all, how many times can I fall in love with my people?" While there is no easy answer to "sharing the wealth," as it were, the relationship between priest and people must not be ignored as irrelevant. Yet that is what is happening all too often.

Similarly, there is no easy answer to how a priest builds this relationship with his people either. Perhaps he needs a small group of trusted people with whom he can share himself more comfortably. Since most parishes are too big for intimacy with everyone, and the situation is getting worse, he may try to do what Jesus did: call some chosen people around him for the sake of all the people. The purpose is not to build his ego or to provide an outlet for recreation, but to have some people who will truly understand him and with whom he can dream his dreams. If anything, they would be like the apostles and holy women were to Jesus.

It is especially important that they be truly strong people of living faith. So much of a priest's time is spent ministering to the weak and the lost sheep of his flock that he needs to be nourished and renewed by them. The priest's good will here is not the issue, but his survival. If he is not being filled up himself, he will eventually try to give from his emptiness. The predictable consequence is burnout. A priest needs strong people around him who know his heart.

While some may see these people in terms of a support group, the level of intimacy demanded seems to call for more than that. They must be willing to experience several facets of the Christian life together. The image of disciples comes to mind, but some may see that as too strong. Nevertheless, a priest needs people with whom he can share prayer and his experience of God. He also needs to hear their stories of faith and what is happening in their spiritual journeys. There needs to be a level of mutual trust that frees them to be accountable to one another as well. Because of the bonding in faith they share, it is not unrealistic to expect them to find ways to reach out to others, to empower them to live the commandment of love. Finally, and by no means least importantly, it is necessary for the priest and his special people to have fun together. If this dimension is lacking in a serious relationship, those involved are not serious enough about it.

The benefits of this kind of intimacy will not only affect a priest personally but also his relationship with all his people. This truth, which is something of a principle in relationships, is clearly demonstrated in marriage. When a husband and wife are strong in their relationship, it positively affects the relationship they have with their family. Even the business world has acknowledged that those who are happily married are also more successful on the job. Some businesses have even sponsored workshops to strengthen the family life of their employees. Celibates need to strengthen their "family life" too.

Healthy Friendships

The question inevitably surfaces about the advisability of a special friendship a priest may have with an individual person. Where does it fit into the picture of his celibate commitments? Of all that can be said on this subject, the core issue for a celibate is the effect it is having on the committed relationship he has with his people. One thing is certain: should it cross over the line and become an exclusive relationship, there is no way a celibate priest can remain faithful to his people.

The problem for the celibate, then, is how he can discern whether or not a special friendship he has is truly healthy. Dr. Teresita Scully, a professional counselor and spiritual director, makes some helpful observations. She says that any real friendship is going to involve intimacy, time, and affection. After mentioning that many of our saints had intimate friendships, like Francis and Clare, Teresa and John, and Jerome and Paula, she says, "To deny intimacy or its importance in our spiritual growth is to deny the very nature of God's manner of relating to us."[3] Time, though necessary, is not in itself an indication a friendship is healthy. It may or may not be. Dr. Scully urges withholding negative judgments. Regarding affection, she continues,

> The celibate's love for friends, be they of the same or opposite sex, religious or clerical, single or married, is no different from love between married persons, except in its expression (nongenital). It is pursuing a mirage to look for "spiritual" love as if it did not involve the same feelings as any other human love."[4]

Having said this, Dr. Scully then poses five questions a celibate must honestly and objectively answer either to himself or his spiritual director(s):

1. "What effect is this relationship having on my ability to reason?" If one finds himself defending his friend without objectivity, something may be wrong.

2. "What effect is it having on my community relationships?" If a priest is not becoming more loving toward his people, or if he is becoming uninterested in those close to him, or is not listening to them, something unhealthy may be happening.

3. "What effect is this relationship having on my activities?" If a priest is looking for ways to get out of his duties in order to have more time with his friend, a red flag should go up. A celibate relationship should not include actions that are only appropriate for those who are married or have that option open to them. If the actions become clandestine, they go against the very nature of bearing witness, an important part of every healthy relationship. Friendship, an aspect of Christian love, should not be concealed.

4. "Does your friendship involve feelings of jealousy?" If a priest feels jealous or resents it when others get close to his friend, it is a sign that he sees that person as someone to possess, not love. "Love is not jealous" (I Cor. 13:4).

What these celibate friendships will look like is something
each priest must work out in his particular situation. It is
worth mentioning again that for a celibate to live his celibacy fully, he must do so in the atmosphere of living faith.
Only if his relationship with God is strong can he acquire a
clear perspective on his special friendships. Father George
A. Aschenbrenner, S.J., offers his perspective on this subject as follows:

> In every human heart there is a desire for a marital
> mate, and every man and woman enjoys a God-given
> seductiveness. Of course, this seductive tendency can
> be misused to corrupt healthy human relationships,
> but its presence is healthy in itself and can promote
> something much more valuable than simple mating: a
> vision of the whole human family as bonded in ma-
> ture, enjoyable, loving relationships. The celibate's
> aim must not be to suppress or destroy this natural
> tendency, but to understand it and then to carefully
> adapt his or her expression of it.[5]

On a broader scale, it seems a priest needs to find ways to
share more from his heart in his homilies. In this way, all his
people will get to know him to some degree. In any case, he
will have to fight the temptation to hide behind the protec-
tion of ministry. He knows that as long as the people focus
on his activities they will not focus on him. Should they be
displeased with what he is doing, his saving strategy can
always be to do it better or to do something else. In either
case, he would not become vulnerable by revealing himself
to them. A committed celibate cannot continue to believe
that as long as he does good things his people will be satisfied with him. Covenant relationships require more. After
all, his title "Father" is not meant to keep people at a distance but to invite them to intimacy. Yet the thought of
intimacy with his people is not all that attractive to many
priests.

A hesitant priest's reasoning may be much like that which

Father John Powell, S.J., uses in his books, *Why Am I Afraid to Tell You Who I Am?* and *Why Am I Afraid to Say I Love You?*. He writes, "I am afraid to tell you who I am, because, if I tell you who I am, you may not like who I am, and it's all that I have."[6] The fear of rejection by many a priest is real. When he steps out from behind his activities, he is exposed to the judgments of his people. He opens himself to rejection. If they do not like him, his vulnerability opens him to genuine hurt, and the pain is real. This is why priests, not unlike many married persons, hesitate to reveal who they really are even to the most important people in their lives. That is why mutual love has to be the foundation of a celibate's relationship with his people. If a priest does not sense he is loved, he will not reveal himself to his people. Without being loved, there is no chance of any real depth of relationship between priest and people.

The Celibate's Need to Be Loved

The degree of knowledge a priest and his people have of one another will determine the potential depth of their love for one another. But like the act of self-revelation, the depth of their love is a decision they have to make. Living celibacy, then, like living marriage, requires constant effort. There is nothing automatic about it. The way one lives today sets the stage for the way he will live tomorrow. While it is relatively easy for a priest to love his people, it takes a greater effort to receive their love in return. When he is loving, it is on his terms; he is in control. But when he is receiving love, he must give up control and allow his people to love him on their terms. Even though his people's devotion to him is the best support his celibacy can possibly have, it is common for a priest to deny them this opportunity.

Too many priests are simply not accessible to their people.

They cannot be reached or they treat their people more like clients than family. Some priests refuse to visit their people or even share a meal in their homes. While the advent of lay ministers has been a positive development in most parishes, they may have actually distanced priests that much further from their people. Even though this reluctance for intimacy may be passed off as just a typical masculine defect, it is not so innocent. If priests are not allowing their people to get close enough to love them, how can they really be celibates at all? Without an openness to receive love, they simply cannot be living in a love relationship with their people.

Priests often have an uncanny way of protecting themselves from getting too close to anyone. Parishioners are made to feel guilty if they call outside of office hours. They know how "busy" Father is. At times he is almost impossible to reach. As though answering services were not enough, some priests do not let their people know where they can be reached when they are "off duty" at home. The message comes through loud and clear. "Do not disturb!" And as long as this is true, the priest-people relationship will be on the priest's terms. This makes loving him pretty hard. Some people have simply given up, either from frustration or hurt. While they may sadly pass it off as a fact of life in the "modern" church, that does not lessen the emptiness in their hearts that comes from not getting through to their priest. Whether he realizes it or not, he comes across as so superior, so unreal, so busy that getting close to his people is never an issue with him. The only time he seems to care is when someone comes to him with a problem.

Even when the faithful admire their priest and are truly grateful for his efforts in their behalf, without a sense of devoted love from him no sacrifice he makes will lead them to an enthusiasm of heart for him. He has made it too hard. As a people, their needs for love, belonging, self-esteem, and the freedom to be themselves have not been met in their relationship with him. After all, enthusiasm of heart comes from being a friend, not a client.

While this reluctance for intimacy may be due to past hurts, more commonly priests are simply embarrassed about calling forth love toward themselves. Some may even see it as something selfish on their part, when in reality it is not that at all. It allows the flow of love to move back and forth between priest and people. In fact, this is when the church operates best, when it is most personal and real, when it is closest to the way Jesus operated with the apostles and holy women. He asked them two significant questions. "Who do you say that I am?" and, "Do you love me?" It was important that they knew him. It was necessary that they loved him. These are also basic questions for a priest to ask, not for his personal aggrandizement but for the unity of his parish. Unless the priest loves and is loved, his parish is not united. This is getting to the heart of why celibacy is important to the church. It calls forth this kind of love.

Can you imagine the reaction of parishioners if their priest were to ask them from the pulpit, "Do you love me?" They would be shocked, no doubt, but also delighted. If they do not hear it, it may be because their priest would rather be respected than loved. It is "safer" that way. Or maybe he would rather be needed than loved. After all, being a problem solver or do-gooder is "safer" too. Yet that same priest, who is scandalized to hear of children growing up in his parish who have never heard their father say, "I love you," is totally oblivious to the fact that his own people have never heard him say, "I love you" to them — and they call him "Father" every day. This certainly makes saying, "I love you" in return much more difficult. If a priest loves his people, why should he not tell them? With some exceptions, most parishioners truly want to love their priests. They are even predisposed to love them. They need only to be given a little encouragement.

Somehow, sooner or later, this unwillingness to place one-self in the hands of one's beloved must be exposed for what it is, an American middle-class attitude. Independence is valued above relationship. This attitude is not found in the Gospel anywhere. It is void of faith. Yet the faithful are calling their priests to commit themselves to them in faith. When this is shown, even in the simplest ways, they the faithful will respond too. After all, on the day of ordination, a priest was not just entrusted with the Eucharist, the Body of Christ; he was also entrusted with the baptized people, the Body of Christ. Each Sunday a priest trusts his people enough to place the Eucharist in their hands. Why is he so reluctant to place himself in their hands too? Of course it takes faith, great faith. It is only the empowerment of the Holy Spirit that can enable a priest to have the love and trust of an *alter Christus*. Yet this is the way celibacy is calling a priest to live.

The Temptation

The temptation in many parishes, therefore, is to settle for fellowship, which requires only a getting along. It places a minimal demand on relationship. Since it does not require a depth of belonging, the strength of commitment expected among the people is not very high. Rather than seeing unity as intimate belonging, a positive force in a parish, it is seen only as freedom from divisions. Hopping from parish to parish is accepted as a fact of life for priest and people. Peaceful coexistence is often an acceptable compromise to maintain fellowship. Therefore, when fellowship is all a community is looking for in terms of relationship, celibacy is seen as irrelevant. What need is there to accept the celibate challenge to go all the way when settling for minimums is perfectly acceptable?

When fellowship is accepted as the model for belonging in

a community, a parish will be judged as good or bad in terms of the opportunities it offers the people to exercise their talents, or in terms of how up to date it is, or how sensitive it is to the issues some hold dear. It would be like judging the strength of a marriage in terms of how talented a husband and wife are, or how involved they are in civic affairs or in touch with the latest social trends. Unfortunately, such things do not say a word about the couple's relationship, and marriage is about relationship. So is the church. That alone is the primary standard to judge the strength of a community of faith. While parish activities are important, they are not as important as what is happening between the people themselves as a result of those activities. Is their unity expressed and growing because of their mutual love? That is the dynamic that will give credibility to a community's activity. While fellowship is good, the Gospel calls for more from the followers of Christ. Personal integrity is also good, but it takes more than that if the church is to be a living organism. Jesus did not command us to get along but to love one another as he loved us. "This is how all will know you for my disciples" (John 13:35).

Diversity in Community

The fact that parishes are composed of all kinds of people is not a threat to this unity at all. It is a mistake to think that a strong community will be composed of those people who think alike and agree on everything. Diversity is, in fact, a great asset to a parish. Community and individuality are not opposites. They can both exist at the same time. After all, the ultimate model of community is the Trinity. God is one and community at the same time. Strong individuals make for strong communities. If those who make up a community are weak, so too will be the community. While one may be emphasized from time to time, individuality and community are both needed. Since there is always going to be tension between these two poles, balance between them is essential. If one is overemphasized, both will eventually suffer. Excessive individualism weakens community and deprives people of their need for others. (Is this why loneliness is so common in our society today?) Conversely, excessive conformity weakens individuals and eventually destroys community. (Is this not the breeding ground of revolution or a Jonestown tragedy?)

As mentioned earlier, the human model for community is the married couple. When both husband and wife are healthy individuals, they have a good running start at a healthy marriage. So when a couple married fifteen years claim they have never had an argument, one would be advised not to assume they have a healthy marriage. Either one spouse dominates the other, or they are both afraid of "rocking the boat." When differences arise, and they do, "peace at any price" takes over. The price is often high in terms of frustration, distrust, or fear. That is neither healthy for the two people as individuals nor for their marital relationship. Both parties have unique gifts to bring to their relationship that affect the quality of their marriage. This diversity of gifts must be encouraged. The same is true in the church community.

Diversity in membership is a good running start for a strong community. If all the people are alike, the community may well be shallow. It is not insignificant that Jesus chose very different people to follow him, from ordinary fishermen to zealots, from religious leaders to outcasts. There is no scandal that Paul would eventually oppose Peter. What Jesus was saying was that discipleship was offered to all. No one was to be excluded from his invitation to share in his "common meal." This was, of course, in direct violation to the caste system and a major affront to the privileged classes, especially to the religious establishment. This was also the basis of the persecutions the early church suffered at the hands of the Roman emperors. Christianity offered full participation in life to whoever wanted it. Rather than being a threat to the Roman gods, Christianity was a threat to Roman social structures. That is what bothered the emperors. Should this notion spread, they reasoned, the empire would be through. The early Christians were persecuted for being good Christians. From their diversity they formed a community strong enough to threaten the mightiest empire in the world. Unlike the situation in so many churches today, the early church realized its purpose as a community was not to change the individuals who belonged, but to change itself as a community through a committed, mutual love of those who formed it.

Jesus' Call to Communion

Jesus did not spend much of his energy ministering to the people who would be his church. He actually served the apostles and holy women very little. When we consider the famous scene during the Last Supper when he washed the feet of the disciples, it is necessary to understand the meaning of that gesture in those days. It was an act of courtesy and hospitality. True to form, the disciples had just been arguing and were at odds. By washing their feet, Jesus provided a model of how all his disciples are to live with one another. Forgiveness had to be central to their life together.

But even if we view this incident as symbolic of service, the fact is that the normal dealings Jesus had with the holy women and apostles were not in terms of what he did for them. His ministry was primarily to others. To those who would be his church, he offered intimacy with himself and his Father. In doing so, he also offered them a life of communion with one another. In fact, he prays that this communion will extend to his followers for all time. "I do not pray for them alone. I pray also for those who will believe in me through their word, that all may be one as you, Father, are in me, and I in you; I pray that they may be one in us, that the world may believe that you sent me" (John 17:20–21). This is not a prayer for those who will simply believe in Jesus, but for those who will believe in the Jesus as revealed by the people of the church. This calls for intimacy within the church. Believing in Jesus is dependent on the credibility of our intimacy.

Communion in the Eucharist

It is not by coincidence that Jesus washed the disciples' feet and prayed for unity in the church on the evening of the Last Supper. It was then that he gave the Eucharist, the great sacrament of unity, to the church. This gift was to become the source and center of church life. As the Second Vatican Council declared when speaking of the Eucharist, "The liturgy is the summit toward which the activity of the Church is directed; at the same time it is the fountain from which all her power flows" (*Constitution on the Sacred Liturgy*, no. 10). This means that the Christian life in all its expressions relates in some way to the eucharistic celebration. The Eucharist is more than just a nice touch to the church's life; it is at its core. As noted earlier, liturgy is to the life of the church what sexual intercourse is to marriage. This means that what genital intimacy is to a married couple, the Eucharist is to the faithful. Each Eucharist is a celebration of an existing reality, flowing from the unique relationship of the people involved. Each Eucharist is also intended to deepen that relationship. It is at the core of that relationship. In fact, just as the sexual relationship of the married couple can serve as a barometer of the couple's overall relationship, so the place of the Eucharist in the life of the faithful can serve as a barometer of the faithful's overall relationship with one another. In either case, should the relationship break down, the "celebration" reverts to a meaningless activity or empty ritual.

As leader in the faith community, this is a priest's major concern. The place of the Eucharist in his life is critical. Just as the honeymoon does not last forever, neither does the first enthusiasm of priesthood. While a priest's familiarity with the Eucharist does not breed contempt, it may breed a certain kind of complacency. Celebrating Mass can become a duty to perform for one's people, something to "get through" in the easiest possible way. Rather than seeing it as an expression of the unity of the church in Jesus, with the focus on what is happening to the people, it can become an opportunity to experiment with the latest liturgical innovations, regardless of what the people may think. Performance replaces sensitive communication and communion. The guide to good liturgy becomes the latest manual describing "how to do it." While this may be a bit exaggerated, the parallels implied with the attitudes some have about sex are intended. This does not mean that the priest has lost faith in the Eucharist itself, but that he may have lost touch with his people.

Since the Eucharist is central to the life of the church, it is understandable why the quality of relationship that exists among its people is so significant. What intimacy is to the married couple, communion is to the faithful. The way a couple lives with each other will affect the sexual celebration of their intimacy. The way the faithful live with one another will profoundly affect the eucharistic celebration of their communion. It is this communion with one another that a priest of today has to offer his people. This is his primary role as a priest. As leader of the eucharistic celebration, he invites his people to unity with one another and with the Father through Jesus. His focus is not on changing individuals to a certain conformity of thought or devotion but on forming a community of love where unique gifts are acknowledged and celebrated. It is not incidental, therefore, that he as priest is committed to living in communion with them himself.

The Celibate Witness

A priest's closeness to his people, however, is not so that others will think of how self-sacrificing he is but how lovable and worthy of love they are. The priest witnesses to that warmth, closeness, affection, and honesty that should characterize the relationship that exists among the members of the Body of Christ with one another. Celibacy, then, is not meant just to help the priest meet his human emotional needs. It is also meant to help the people of the church grow in their love for one another. When they see how their priest sees them, loves them, forgives them, praises them, in their strengths and weaknesses, in their diversity of gifts, they will begin to see themselves through his eyes, as it were. Even when he has to challenge or confront them, he does so because he sees a greatness in them they are not seeing or living up to. In a sense, a priest is called to bring out the beauty in his people so they can see it too. By his love, he invites them to communion with one another. He gathers them around himself and the Eucharist each week, if not daily, for this reason.

Evaluating a Parish

The evaluation of a parish therefore begins with what is going on between the priest and his people. Is there a real communion between them? Do the people really love their priest? Granted, the evaluation does not end here, since the church is to proclaim Christ in a believable way to the world. This requires a genuine love between the people too. From their communion flows the mission of the church. The issue is real love between a priest and people, not sentimentality. It is not a matter of whether they *like* their priest, but whether they *love* him. Do they see him as their bridegroom or as their servant bachelor? Often parishioners will like their priests, but there is no real closeness. They like the fact that he is up to date, theologically balanced, does the right things, or gives good homilies. But this says nothing about love. Unfortunately, priests seem to prefer it this way. It is just too embarrassing otherwise. Objective standards are far less threatening.

It would be interesting to watch the reaction of priests if their bishop were to ask them in the annual parish report, "How loved are you by your people?" What if a parish council evaluated its pastor in terms of his love for the parishioners and then the parishioners in terms of their tenderness of heart toward him? Why not ask questions like these? St. John of the Cross did say, "In the evening of life, we will be judged on love." Considering the all-too-common distance, anticlericalism, poor sacerdotal morale, and dissatisfaction that exists in the priest-people relationship today, there must be some way to foster and encourage closeness and warmth. The fact is that people will forgive and excuse almost anything for somebody they love. Not love in the sense of letting their priest do his own thing but in the sense of being close, affectionate, warm, and tender. This is not a new idea. St. Paul expressed it long ago. "Love one another with the affection of brothers" (Rom. 12:10). When this kind of love is genuine, the faithful will be in a good position to challenge their priest to grow without being accused of being anticlerical.

A Radical Departure

Just as a married man must evaluate his success as a husband in terms of how happy his wife is, a celibate priest must evaluate his success as a celibate in terms of how happy his people are. Again, the focus is not self but his beloved. A priest should look at his people and have them tell him how their life is more joyful because of his love for them, and because he has accepted their choice of him as their own. This is the basis of the witness-value of celibacy. It is not meant to witness to a priest's dedication, heroism, or martyrdom, but to the people's own beauty and goodness by the depth of belonging he has with his people that is characterized by affection and tenderness. Ultimately it is a witness to Jesus who drew people to himself because of his open display of love and affection for them. If this is a new way of being a priest for some, so be it. Priests and their people can change. It is no less critical for them than it is for married couples who need to change to rekindle the love between them. Furthermore, it is no less possible.

If this seems like a radical departure from the normal way of thinking about celibacy, that is because it is. There has been entirely too much focus on what the celibate gives up and on what he cannot do. Celibacy has been cast in such a negative light that it has been almost impossible to see any real value it offers the church in terms of proclaiming the Gospel and announcing the Kingdom. How can anyone expect celibacy to do any proclaiming of anything as long as it is seen as an avoidance of relationship and, therefore, a negative life experience? If all that can be said in favor of celibacy is that it frees the priest to work more for the institutional church, that in fact is an admission that celibacy is exploitative and cruel. There is absolutely nothing about such thinking that calls attention to the Lord's intervention in life. This is not an overstatement. Jesus and his message need to be presented by attractive people — people whom others want to be with, people who exhibit a joy in their relationships. This is what is most attractive about the church. We are called by Jesus to be a communion of people. Celibacy, as a charism of the Spirit, gives hope that this will happen. In fact, it is this sense that celibacy best proclaims the Kingdom of God. Rather than just pointing to another world, or to something in the future that will come, it points to the reality of that Kingdom as it exists now in the lives of those living in a communion of peace and love with one another.

The Faithful as Spouse

Contrary to popular thought, a priest cannot live celibacy alone. He cannot even be celibate without someone else with whom he can share a love-relationship. Therefore, it is necessary for the faithful to realize that their priests need them if they are going to live the charism of celibacy at all. Not only must they call the priest to celibacy, they must also sustain his celibacy by their love for him. Regardless of what some may think about the whole issue of a married clergy, there are priests today who have pledged themselves to live their lives for the church as celibates. They cannot be dismissed as a dying breed. They need others. In an analogous way, the people of the church are to live as their spouse. This requires more than cordiality or a love of benevolence. It requires a commitment of love beyond attraction and sentiment, a readiness to belong, for better or worse, for richer or poorer, in sickness and in health.

The faithful are to be partners in the celibacy of their priest and to share it with him in a personal way. They cannot be indifferent to his celibacy but must make it known how they have a stake in the quality of the priest-people relationship too. In a very real way, their priest's ability to live celibacy is in their hands. They must be ready to share how their lives are enriched because of their celibate's relationship with them, and how they believe their relationship together as people and priest gives life to the rest of the Body of Christ. People need to tell their priests that they believe celibacy is not just a regulation. There is no place for implying their lives are wasted because they cannot marry.

In a sense, of course, they are married, but certainly not with the exclusivity that exists between a man and woman. But the warmth, sensitivity, and commitment are just as real. For this reason, a priest's people need to experience his involvement with them rather than just being the objects of his service. They need to be loved by him, belong to him, feel valued by him, and sense the freedom to choose to give themselves to him in a loving way. Just as couples know how important it is to be acknowledged as sacraments of the church, especially in terms of going beyond their own personal limitations to be more for each other, priests and people need to experience the same kind of empowerment by one another. The people must be ready to thank their priests for accepting their invitation to belong to them by living a celibate way of life. And priests must be ready to thank their people for accepting them as the center of their community of faith.

Supporting Celibacy

When such loving trust is present, the people will show their concern for their priests even when it may be awkward or difficult to do so. For instance, married couples know people who will nurture their coupleness, and others who will encourage their independence from each other instead. Therefore, as with their children, they cannot take the people with whom they associate lightly. Similarly, caring people should let their priest know how important it is to them whom he associates with. They cannot be afraid to ask if he is regularly with people who support and nurture his celibacy, who affirm him, who call and challenge him to a life of relationship. After all, a priest does this very same thing out of concern for his people. Why should they not do it out of concern for him?

Certainly priests need to be with their brother priests, not just on days off but also for mutual support and encouragement. Jesu Caritas and Emmaus Groups serve this purpose very well. But it would be a mistake if they did not spend quality time with lay people as well, especially those living the values of committed relationships on a daily basis. It is important that priests be close to healthy married couples with whom they can share themselves honestly and openly. Some priests may even be inclined to develop an intimate, close relationship with a devoted married couple and to act in the capacity of a spiritual director for them. This will draw on the intimate connection of the two sexual life experiences, giving the priest healthy exposure to a committed sexual love that is uniquely ecclesial. It will also expose him to the advice and direction of women who love men, and of men who have a unique devotion to and responsiveness toward women. This is a much-needed resource in our church today. It will also help him avoid the trap of excessive professionalization and self-identification based upon accomplishment. The clarity and simplicity of the couple's devotion to each other will be a real enhancement to his own simplicity and commitment. As well as anybody, they can spot any tendency a priest may have to withdraw from his people and begin to settle for the independence of a bachelor.

Specifically, a priest could pick the holiest couple he knows who have a real grasp of their sacrament of matrimony and the dynamics of relationship. He would come to them for direction in terms of how he is living out his relationship with his people. Attention would not be on his ministerial skills but on his personal life, such as prayer, spirituality, and how he approaches liturgies and homilies. The issue is not how well he does them but the mentality he projects toward the people when celebrating Mass or giving a homily. What is his mentality toward women, brother priests, his bishop, or his blood family? Is he affirming of others? Does he show affection? Does he allow people to get close to him? Is he willing to be a prophet for his people, challenging them to live the full Gospel? Is he willing to risk for them? This is the kind of agenda his couple would focus on. They could do wonders in calling him to growth. While many priests would be hesitant to try this, most priests would be surprised at just how perceptive some couples are and how helpful they can be in terms of relationship. But if love is present, there is no reason to fear.

Furthermore, this is immensely practical since celibacy and matrimony are two lifestyles that mutually support and reinforce each other. By being close to truly sacramental couples, a celibate will experience and discover many key elements in the dynamics of human relationships that will strengthen his relationship with his people. The principles a husband and wife must live to remain close as a couple are the same a celibate must live with his people. For example, when there are tensions, hurts, or differences, reaching out toward the other, rather than running away, is what is called for. The need for reconciliation and the healing of hurts is revealed as essential to a lasting relationship. The quality of permanency in the couple's relationship will remind him of the significance of this quality in his relationship with the Body of Christ. He will see that matrimony and celibacy are truly complementary and not in competition. It will help the priest focus on those people to whom he has committed himself, and not concern himself with that someone he could have married. As a husband sees there is simply no place for another woman when he is loving his wife, the priest will see there is no room for an exclusive relationship with anyone else when he is loving his people as a celibate.

But perhaps more than anything, married couples can show a priest by their lives that living in relationships of love with others is at the heart and meaning of life. Couples show this when they selflessly give up material comforts and career advancements for the sake of their relationship; when they believe in their love enough to bring new life into the world, even though it may mean added hardships. They help a priest believe in the power of his love too, and to believe that a depth of relationship is not only necessary, but also possible for him. They help him realize that growth in love is not the result of sprinkling fairy dust around but is the result of much self-giving and hard work. Couples can even teach a priest that his call is to love all his people, not just those whom he happens to like. He cannot pick and choose. After all, a husband cannot just love that part of his wife he likes. He must love her as she is. He cannot love her as she used to be or as he dreams she might be. Only one spouse exists for him to love, the one he has here and now, for better or worse. A priest does not have two spouses either. His spouse is the church as it is. No other church exists — not the one he used to know nor the one he dreams might be. There is no other church to love than the one in his life. A husband loves his wife as she is. A priest can do no less with his people.

The issue here is communion, not fellowship. They are clearly not the same. The telling mark of fellowship is that when we become disenchanted we can walk away. If there is someone we do not like, we can write them off. That is not the way of communion. By communion we are family. We cannot stop being part of family because we disagree. We are bound together by common blood. It is the blood of Jesus that binds us as the family of God. No matter how we try, we keep coming back to the center of our lives as Catholics: the Eucharist.

Three Levels

From all that has been said so far, it becomes apparent that there are three levels at which a priest can evaluate the effectiveness of the charism of celibacy he has been asked to live. The first level is self. Is it helping him meet his needs for love, belonging, self-worth, and autonomy? The second level is the community of faith. Are the people to whom he is committed growing in their love for one another because of his love for them? The third level is the world. Are those outside the church finding his people so attractive and inviting that they are developing a desire to become a part of it? Or, to put it another way, are they experiencing the Kingdom of God in the church?

When we remember that the church exists to proclaim the Good News, it becomes imperative that the spirit that characterizes that community is, in fact, good news. Remembering also that the church is a broken church, made up of sinful people who do not live faith fully or love unconditionally, it is imperative also that the church be a community of hope. Hope rises out of faith and precedes perfect love. Without hope, the union of all things in Christ can never be achieved. Without hope, love will remain only an ideal and will never become that practical force necessary for transforming the world. Even though hope may be an anomaly in our despairing world, it must be an uncompromising characteristic of anyone who has been incorporated into the Body of Christ, the church. But if hope is also an anomaly in the church, or any part of it, there must be something drastically wrong.

7

Despair or Hope?

As the chapter titles in this book suggest, priests facing the challenge of celibacy have a lot of choices to make. Celibacy, in a sense, is at the mercy of those who are called to live it, either as a source of joy or a breeding ground for regrets. They can choose to see it as a privation or a privilege. That choice will determine the fundamental stance they take toward their people, as bachelor or bridegroom, as well as the nature of that relationship itself, as a contract or covenant. Needless to say, their masculine/feminine integration will influence the outcome of each. This, in turn, will set the tone for the way people will experience the church, as a simple fellowship or as a communion of people living in unity. While priests cannot face this challenge alone, inasmuch as the people of the church must accept it too, it is the response of priests that will either encourage or discourage the faithful to take it seriously.

A Positive Desire

In many ways, the attitude of mind and heart that priests bring to celibacy will determine the kind of choices they make. This is why the virtue of hope becomes so important to their priestly life. Not so much hope in the sense of trusting that good will prevail over evil but hope as a desire, a longing for something. It is the difference evidenced in those who trust Christ will return at the end of time and in those who truly long for his return at the end of time. Hope is operative in both groups, but it has a sense of eagerness and yearning to it in the latter group that the first does not enjoy. Rather than being just a state of will, hope in this sense actually influences a person's thinking and behavior. Enthusiasm displaces passivity. There is a big difference between "I trust" and "I can hardly wait."

There is one question that is seldom if ever asked of a person preparing for Orders. "Do you want to be a celibate?" They may be asked if they will accept celibacy, but not if they "want" it. Maybe this is so because the assumed answer will be a resounding "No!" But this is a question that should be asked, especially by those already ordained. "Do I want to be a celibate priest?" If their answer is still a resounding "No!" then soul-searching on their part is in order. They have to find out why and then deal with it in prayerful and careful discernment. But there are those who say "No" who may never have thought of asking for the grace of celibacy. They never thought to because they never understood it enough to want it.

The only thing keeping some priests from living celibacy with joy may be their lack of desire to be celibate. They may be lacking in the virtue of hope as the God-given desire for this charism that will be for the good of themselves, their people, and the church at large. Without the help of God's grace, no priest will have the courage and strength to choose a way of life that is so contrary to the norms of society. He may be able to tolerate it but not really choose it. But priests deserve a better shot at a full and rewarding life than that. After all, if a priest's whole life is based on the foundation of faith, then he should be able to expect God's help to live that life to the fullest. Somehow, he must overcome whatever obstacles to this desire that exist in his life. He must eventually ask for the grace of celibacy.

Pessimism

While there may be many reasons why priests are not enthusiastic about receiving the charism of celibacy, one major one is that hope and optimism are not really in vogue today. It is just so much easier to be a pessimist than an optimist. It is true that for some mysterious reason people seem to pay particular attention to bearers of bad news. Let someone find a mistake, flaw, or fault in a person, project, or plan, and soon he is quoted as an expert on the subject. But let someone else speak to the brighter side of life, and that person is casually dismissed as well-intentioned, perhaps, but naïve. While this may be overstated a bit and hard to prove, it typifies our own experience.

Charles Osgood, an ABC news commentator, made this very same point one day. He even referred to some scientific studies for evidence. People who are inclined to see the negative side of things are usually given more credit for having a better grasp of reality than those who see the positive side of things. Jennifer James, a popular anthropologist in the Seattle area, put it rather bluntly: "Why do we think happy is dumb?" She observes that clowns are regarded as fools. People who smile a lot are suspect. Could it be that people who frown a lot know something the rest of mankind does not? But why is the opposite not also true? Could not a smile be saying, "I know something you don't?"

The assumption behind this phenomenon seems to be that if optimists really knew what was going on, they would not be so happy all the time. (Most pessimists seem bent on making sure they find out.) God knows there is an abundant supply of negative things going on in our society that cannot be ignored. But the truth is that one does not have to be particularly smart to see them. Nor does it take much skill to point out the mistakes, faults, and flaws in others. They abound around us. By objective observation, there seems to be no legitimate reason to believe pessimists are smarter than anyone else. We (and they) just assume they are.

A Choice

If anything, pessimists are really the ones to feel sorry for, not optimists. Pessimists are not born that way. They choose it. For one reason or another, they choose to see the glass as half empty rather than half full. They look at a garden and see the weeds instead of the flowers. They cannot see silver linings, usually because they do not want to. They are conditioned to think in negatives. They relish reading things that support their negative viewpoints. They are comfortable around other negative people and come across as condescending toward those who do not see reality their way. This would not matter except for the sad fact that pessimism spreads. Pessimism begets pessimism. And when pessimism abounds, there is little room for hope.

A Dying Breed

Some pastors, seemingly on the edge of despair, talk about the growing shortage of priests. They are practically paralyzed by the thought of what the situation will be like by the year 2000. The first thing that comes to their minds when they hear the word "priest" is "dying breed." They are often difficult to talk to because their opinions are so strong. They are so confident they are right that they always sound convincing. After all, who can argue with logic based on the negative aspects of the institutional church? It is there for all to see. Sadly, their near-sighted vision does not embrace a broader view of church that could possibly reveal reasons for hope. Instead they reflect a negativism that limits their own creativity. Their gifts are often either paralyzed altogether or spent in finding someone to blame for the situation. Their negativism is even intimidating to those who have hope for the future.

People in despair cannot seem to admit that there may well be a silver lining to this problem, like the emergence of the laity to their rightful place as ministers in the church or the greater and truly pastoral role that priests of the future must take. Unfortunately prophets of doom almost sound infallible. But they do not deserve the credibility they seem to enjoy. Who is to say the priesthood will not become an attractive alternative for young people again? Discussions with despairing priests usually go nowhere, often ending with some charge like, "You've got your head in the clouds." Their despairing attitude not only blinds them to creative ways of addressing the so-called "vocation problem," it also negatively influences the attitudes of others, especially those who might want to consider being priests themselves some day. Ironically, pessimists often perpetuate what they fear the most. (There is also a vocation problem for the sacrament of matrimony. It is not a shortage of numbers, but a shortage of couples actually being called by the church to the vocation of matrimony as a sacramental way of life they are to live for the church.)

Hurts

Pessimism is often the by-product of unhealed hurts. If negative experiences are not dealt with constructively, they become the basis of negative attitudes and, eventually, a pessimistic view of life. When a priest feels taken for granted by his people, or when his special gifts are not taken into account when assigned to a specific parish, a hurt is begun. If they are not healed, it is just that much easier for the priest to focus his attention on his people's weaknesses or his bishop's shortcomings. When a priest is treated with indifference, or when his opinion on diocesan matters is considered irrelevant, again a hurt begins. He can easily develop a negative attitude toward that bastion of intrigue, "the chancery." On other occasions, the hurt may come from being treated only as another minister in the church with no special role in the life of the faithful. Or maybe he is expected to have all the answers to the questions people ask. In any case, his discouragement (or is it disillusionment?) leads him to a negative perspective toward the people in his life and, eventually, life itself.

A Lost Vision

What often happens is that when a priest's picture of reality is so violated and healing does not take place, he loses his vision of the priesthood too. It is as if his dream died. He cannot help wondering what it is all about and becomes a likely candidate for developing a cynical attitude toward his bishop, his people, and even the church itself. When this happens, such a priest is literally a handicapped person. In many ways, he has become blind, lame, and deaf. He can see no reason for hope; he is crippled in his efforts to pursue his vision of priesthood; he cannot even hear the promptings of the Spirit within him. If he does not address these hurts, either to heal or to let them go, things will only get worse. Pessimism will become his way of life.

Choosing Hope

While such persons are, in a sense, victims, they have to take responsibility for their negative attitude. They have no one else to blame since they imposed it upon themselves. It was their choice to deal with their hurts as they did. After all, they were not born that way.

Pessimists and optimists are what they are by choice. Maybe that is why Jesus said "Fear not" so often. The pessimist chooses to live by fear, the optimist by hope. The basis of pessimism is one's choice to focus on the evil that surrounds him. The basis of hope is to focus on that which is good. Despair is looking at the world with a sense of powerlessness. It is battling against insurmountable odds. Hope is looking at the world knowing we are not alone. Jesus promised to be with us always, especially in our struggles. "And know that I am with you always, until the end of the world" (Matt. 28:20). Faith, then, is an important element in this whole discussion. Without faith, we as individuals do stand against insurmountable odds. But with faith, we know we do not stand alone. We not only have the Spirit of Jesus with us, we also stand with those living in that Spirit as well. We have the church.

Jesus' Agenda

Among the People of God, there is no place for despair. This does not mean that God will solve all our problems for us. He promised only to help us solve our problems. It would be a real mistake, therefore, simply to turn our problems over to Jesus for him to solve, as though that were his reason for remaining with us. The contrary is really closer to the truth. Jesus remains on in the world to continue the work he had begun. His ultimate concern is his agenda, not ours. In fact, as his followers, we must make his agenda our own. His "problems" must become our problems. It is his cause that we must be about in the church, not our own. It is his Kingdom that we are trying to proclaim as members of the Body of Christ. To forget this is to lose the only perspective on reality that can give direction to our lives as Christians. Our hopes are tied to his hopes. Our efforts are not to be lessened because we have faith. They are to be increased. Faith allows us to believe that our efforts will not be in vain. Jesus is our reason to hope that the hurt in our lives can be overcome. This is why people with faith have good reason to have an optimistic perspective on life. Faith in Jesus opens the door to hope.

It seems the early Christians had this strong sense of direction. They knew the most important aspect of their lives as the church was their love for one another. Who they were as community was important to them. This is why they were extraordinary. And that is still what will make the church extraordinary today. The so-called "bottom line" of living as followers of Jesus is our love for one another and who we are as community. In the evening of life, we will not be judged on how much we know, but on how we have loved. It will not matter who hurt whom or even why. In fact, the hurts themselves become irrelevant sooner or later. All that will matter is how we chose to deal with those who hurt us. Did we choose to live with them in love or not? Did we even want to?

This is the significance of living with hope. Hope empowers us to risk the experience of love. It gives us the will, the longing for unity again. If it is overcome by despair, the vision of reality that alone comes from love is incomplete. There is no room in one's heart for anyone else, let alone the people of the church. Without love, there is a whole dimension of reality that cannot be experienced. "Intimacy" is just another eight-letter word. Without love, one looks at the world with blind spots. When love is lost, so are dreams. And when dreams are lost, there is nothing left, nothing to hope in. Maybe this is why Jesus commanded his disciples to love one another. It was his only way of insuring that his dreams for the world would not die. This is why following

Jesus' agenda, not our own, must be our paramount concern in the church.

A Critical Question

Married couples are good at keeping a sense of direction in their lives. They know how important it is in their struggles to keep their dreams alive. When rough times come and issues surface that cause hurts between them, like handling money, they know they have to put things in perspective. To help them do this, they need to ask themselves one critical question: "What effect is this issue having on our relationship?" That is always the primary issue. It puts all other issues in proper perspective. In effect, it makes the couple ask, "Is money more important than us?" Even when the situation erupts into a fight, that fight is not so one will win over the other. The couple fights for the sake of their relationship. They cannot allow some issue to divide them. Such fighting is healthy and necessary at times. But whenever they fight out of anger or to put the other down or to win over the other, it is unhealthy. They must stop until they can pull themselves together. They must remind themselves of each other's goodness, that each has a right to speak and to be heard, and that they will not change each other. When a husband and wife care first about their relationship, a good fight will clear the air and reestablish the flow of love between them.

The couple need to remember what things are like when they look at each other with the eyes of love. Their perception of each other is so influenced by their desire to please the other that money is not all that important, even when they disagree about it. Only when a husband and wife can renew their love for each other can they approach the issue of money in a creative and life-giving way. They may never fully agree on the "right way" to handle it, but no matter. Their relationship of love is too important.

Our Vision of Church

In many ways, this book is not primarily about celibacy at all. It is about the vision we have of the church. It is about the nature of that community we call church. It is about how the members of the Body of Christ live with one another. Are we a community of intimacy or not? Do we look at one another with the eyes of love? Unfortunately, it seems that so many of us in the church have become so issue-oriented that we have lost sight of the fundamental issue we must face as church: ourselves and our relationship with one another.

Celibacy is one of these issues. To do it justice, it must be dealt with in this context. As long as celibacy is viewed only as a problem to be solved, the temptation will be to look upon "it" as though it somehow has an existence aside from the people of the church. Sadly this charism, meant for the building up of the church, has become a source of division. It has become just an issue, standing alone like a criminal suspect on trial.

Celibacy in Context

Truly, the issue of celibacy needs to be addressed right along with other issues that confront the church, like the nuclear-arms race, women in the church, the shortage of priests, hunger, and oppression. But what is happening to us because of the celibacy issue may be a symptom of something far more critical we must face as a church: the state of our relationship with one another as members of the Body of

Christ. Because the celibacy question has, in fact, polarized so many in the church, it seems divine counsel alone will guide us through our current malaise. If we cannot address celibacy from a position of mutual trust and love, many possible "solutions" to this complex problem may actually do more harm than good.

Our first concern must be the quality of our love for one another in the church. As the saying goes, "we must not cut off our nose to spite our face." Celibates, especially, must look at the vision they have for their people. How can they best facilitate the implementation of Jesus' agenda for the church today without letting their own personal concerns hinder the process? They need a real desire in their hearts to do this. When they do, they will be sensitive to what is best for the church in terms of its mission of presenting the Gospel of hope to a despairing world. To limit discussion just to the concerns of individual priests or the needs of the institutional church would be an injustice to the charism of celibacy as a gift of the Spirit.

If our vision of church embraces as essential the call to communion, we will ask the same question the married couple does: "What effect is this issue going to have on our relationship as members of the Body of Christ?" Sometimes the answers are not clear; sometimes risks must be taken; sometimes mistakes will be made. Sometimes the problems will be beyond our capacity to solve, at least at the present time. This is no one's fault. It is just a fact of life. Sometimes we will unavoidably hurt one another too, but hurts can be healed. Sometimes we will even end up fighting. That too is okay as long as we are fighting for our relationship with one another, for the sake of the church. "Healthy fights" have a legitimate place in the church. We are not expected to agree on everything. But we cannot afford to fight if it means attacking one another. And from experience, like the married couple, we know we will not change anyone anyhow. We must be willing to see the goodness in one another, listen to one another, and speak honestly what we see to be true from our hearts.

The Goal

This is why it is so vital to remember that our goal as a Christian community is not to change the individuals who make it up but to change the nature of the community itself. In fact, we have already been given divine counsel on how to achieve this: "Love one another as I have loved you" (John 15:12). From all our diversity we are to become a community of love. In this case "winning" is not the name of the game, but our unity with one another is. Only if this is our goal can we go about building the Kingdom of God.

Whatever issues confront the church can be resolved for the good of the church as long as those on the opposing sides are open to be both informed by truth as each expresses it and formed by mutual love as each shows it. When we discuss the issue of celibacy in the church, our first concern is what is going to be best for the church, not as institution, but as a faithful people commissioned to live the values of the Kingdom of God for the sake of the world. This means we must free celibacy from the stigma of being seen as a divisive issue in the church and deal with it on its merits as a charism of the Spirit for the sake of the church.

People's Goodness

The real tragedy of viewing life from a negative perspective is that the goodness of people is simply ignored. In extreme cases it is even denied. Constantly focusing on the dark side of people too often leads to blindness about the bright side.

Yet that bright side, the goodness of people, is never to be denied and is always dangerous to forget. The issue of the goodness of all people is out of the question. We can only proclaim it, remind one another of it, and invite people to live it. But deny it? Never! The issue of our goodness was settled once and for all by the redemptive act of Jesus. He offered himself on the cross out of love for all people. He was totally aware of our sinfulness, but that did not blind him to our goodness. "While we were still sinners, Christ died for us" (Rom. 5:8). Love sees beyond what is dark in all of us.

Unfortunately the darkness of negativism is present in the church. While people may disagree with regard to the extent of its influence, its very presence among us to any degree deserves a more creative response than mere toleration. There is too much good in the church to have it upstaged by what is wrong. This is not an appeal to put our heads in the sand and pretend we do not have faults and failings that must be corrected. It is just that pointing out weaknesses will not make them go away. If we are to overcome them, our strategy must be to strengthen what is good about us. "Detest what is evil, cling to what is good" (Rom. 12:9). That is St. Paul's strategy. He pleads, "Do not be conquered by evil but conquer evil with good" (Rom. 12:21). It is because of the unquestioned goodness of the people of the church, the Body of Christ, that this kind of hope is possible. If we believe in our fundamental goodness and in the help of God's grace, we cannot help but be optimistic.

Taking Responsibility

The fact is we are not helpless victims of the evil around us. We have to take responsibility for some of it. If there is a negative atmosphere in the church, it is because we of the church have created it. We cannot blame those who are not Catholic. If we are not breathing in the fresh breeze of the Spirit, if love is not our hallmark, we have no one to blame but ourselves. This is good news, not bad, since it is within our power to change if we choose to. Again, we are back to the issue of our desire to do so. If the antirelationship atmosphere we breath in the church is choking us, we can choose to make living in relationship with our people a top priority. The fact is we are a sinful church. The issue is how are we going to approach our sinfulness, with despair or hope? With pessimism ("They deserve it") or with optimism ("Things don't have to be this way")? With condemnation or forgiveness? What do we want to do? Our answer to the last question is the key to our answer to the others.

Sins against Celibacy

Closely related to this is another interesting question: What sins are most often committed against celibacy? Before answering, keep a few things in mind. Celibacy is inexorably linked to the church and how we of the church are living with one another. Celibacy makes sense only in the context of the church community. In the celibacy debate, celibacy is not the ultimate issue at all. We are, as Catholics. If we are not concerned with our relationship with one another as Catholics, there is no way celibacy, as a charism to foster that relationship, is going to make much difference. In light of this, here is something to think about. If celibacy were abolished today, how many Catholic people would it affect personally? With the exception of those who might want to marry a priest, an educated guess says the percentage would be predictably small. If so, it would betray both our lack of appreciation for who we are as a church and for the charism of celibacy.

With that reminder, take a few moments to answer the following question: What sins are most often committed against celibacy? Be careful. Take a few moments. The obvious answers are not so obvious anymore. They are not sins of illicit sexual behavior or actions that could lead to it. The sins against celibacy are those sins that weaken or destroy the bonds of relationship among people. These are the very same sins that destroy friendships, families, marriages, and parish communities. They are not unique to celibates at all. Furthermore, they may be committed by celibates or against celibates. Even the faithful of the church can sin against celibacy!

Any sin that breeds a negative, antirelationship atmosphere in the church can be a sin against celibacy. While there are many, a few stand out as particularly damaging. They are abiding anger, criticism, pride, apathy, and irresponsibility. These are serious sins against celibacy because they weaken and/or destroy healthy relationships between a priest and his people. When such things are going on, there is no way a priest will find the celibate way of life attractive. He might just as well live as a bachelor. Furthermore, his parishioners will not really care.

Both the priest and his people, however, must take responsibility for the consequences of these sins. They not only break the spirit of hope, they also breed pessimism in the community of faith, deadening the spirit of hope. The vital energy of a parish is actually drained away when people are harboring anger or are looking for faults to expose. Community becomes a delusion as soon as independence becomes a priest's dream, or when its members give up on loving, or just sit back and wait for someone else to make it all work.

Free-floating Hostility

Abiding anger can take many forms. It is usually caused by some unhealed hurt or a life of frustration. Some priests seem to be chronically angry with their people. At times it takes the form of cynicism, and at other times it becomes a kind of free-floating hostility. For example, a priest may be upset with the personnel board of his diocese because of the way his assignment was handled. He judges his desires were ignored and he ends up in an assignment he did not want. The frustration and anger he feels toward the board may actually be projected onto his people. He is cynical in his comments about them, feels no personal commitment to them, and looks forward to being away from them. He may do a good job for them, but when his job is done he is impossible to reach, and he wants it that way. The people feel it too and wonder, "Why doesn't Father like us?" The answer is that they were sent a priest who was harboring an anger he either refused to deal with or did not know how to deal with constructively.

In this example, and there could be others, the fact of the hurt is not questioned. The priest may well have been treated unjustly. It is his reaction to the hurt that is questioned. If he is harboring anger toward the personnel board, he must realize it is spreading like an infection and limiting his relationship with his people. He must either seek reconciliation with the board or let go of the hurt itself. The major stumbling block is his desire to move beyond it. With the grace of hope, he can choose to. But seeking that grace is his first decision to make.

Sometimes the tables are turned, as when a priest is the object of his people's criticism. The tragedy here is that while he may still be a minister to them, he cannot enter into a priestly relationship with them. This is also often the result of an unhealed hurt, either inflicted by the priest himself or even a predecessor. But inflicting hurt in return is not a very loving response. It effectively paralyzes the healing process. There is bound to be a hollow ring to their sharing the Eucharist together. And yet criticism is practically a way of life in some parishes. It is like a cancer that eats away at a man's goodness. A priest's self-worth is the first victim of criticism, followed immediately by his need to belong. (There is no such thing as constructive criticism. There is simply no way to tear someone down "constructively." Correction is something else entirely, since it is a mutually agreed-upon effort to help someone grow. Criticism, which is aimed at the person himself, not his behavior, is never wanted.) If the curse of criticism, which hangs over far too many parishes, were lifted, the morale in those parishes would improve overnight.

But again the same question has to be asked. Do we really want to stop criticizing one another? Do we have a real desire to live in unity as the Body of Christ? Are we willing to look at the good side of the people in our lives, for reasons to affirm and praise them? What is our openness to the changes the virtue of hope will bring?

Anticlericalism

Pride is also a sin against celibacy. It says in its own way, "I do not need you any more. I can get along quite well without you." While there is a certain arrogance to this, the heart of the sin is the desire for independence. By definition, independence is antirelationship. It is not really freedom but half-freedom. It is only freedom from something, not freedom for something. It is not Christian freedom at all. This is true of the priest who wishes to isolate himself from his people, but it is also true for people who do not want to be bothered with having a priest around. In recent years, this form of pride has worn the face of anticlerical-ism. Granted, there is a form of clericalism that is undesir-able, but priests in general are unjustly lumped together as undesirable by some. This form of pride is at least a first cousin to anger, since many who are anticlerical are also carrying around a lot of anger. At best, priests are tolerated because they are needed to celebrate Mass. (Of course there are those who refuse to have a priest even for that.) While this may be a striking demonstration of displeasure with church practice, it does little to heal or build community.

The question these people must ask is, "Do I want to belong to the church, or just to 'my' church?" As Catholics, they cannot have it both ways. It may be a tough decision for some to make, but it has to be made. There is no way they can support celibacy and be anticlerical at the same time. Priests must decide between celibacy and indepen-dence. They cannot have it both ways. Which do they want most? The sad truth is that if they do not desire to live as celibates, they will not. Celibacy requires their free choice to belong.

Apathy goes one step further than pride. It says, "I give up." "I no longer choose to love you." "As far as I am concerned, you no longer exist." It is giving up on love, the very heart of the Gospel message. Without love, there can be no community in the Christian sense. Yet priests are guilty of this when they write off certain segments of their parish. A priest who will only be a priest to the wealthy, or even the poor for that matter, has slipped into this sin. When a hurt has preceded the apathy, it means that reconcil-iation has been rendered impossible. Healing is stopped. Forgiveness is irrelevant. Such a community will always be crippled, since some of its members have been either para-lyzed or cut off entirely. Tragically, such apathy directed toward priests has led to the drifting of some of our people away from the church altogether. And when a priest feels his people have given up on him, he often has nobody to turn to and no place to go.

Those caught in the deathtrap of apathy have no place to turn to but the Gospel itself. The choice is radical. Do they want to live it or not? They have the most fundamental choice to make as Christians: to love or not to love. If they struggle with this decision, it may mean that they lack the desire to choose love, that they have lost hope. It is only when they open themselves to this grace that they can be freed from this trap.

Finally, people sin against celibacy when they refuse to take responsibility for their part in the priest-people relationship. It makes no difference how committed their priest may be to them; if they refuse to respond to him with genuine love and affection, he cannot live a celibate way of life with them. Celibacy takes both priest and people working together at the relationship. If the only thing parishioners want is a priest "to say Mass for them," they have reduced him to a functionary. They must be open to him as a man with human emotional needs for love, belonging, self-worth, and autonomy. They are in the best position to help him meet these needs. It is worth noting, by the way, that they frequently violate their priest's need for autonomy by expecting him to be someone he is not. Comparisons with former pastors, preachers, administrators, and even Jesus can be very irresponsible. When a new priest moves into a parish, he must be allowed to be himself. He deserves to be loved as he is. His people must take responsibility for helping him feel this freedom to be himself with them.

But this does not just happen automatically. The people must make the decision to be responsible. Do they want just a functionary priest or a priest who will be a part of their lives? Are they willing to accept their priest as he is? To love him as he is? If they are lacking this desire, they must open their hearts to God's gift of hope.

Paternalism

Paternalism is another example of irresponsibility. In this case, the priest keeps tight control over everything and ends up treating his people like children. There is no adult-to-adult relationship between them. The priest looks down on his people, refusing them the opportunity to use and develop their gifts and talents for the sake of the church. Rather than being a life-giver to his people, he actually frustrates them. He does nothing to nurture their sense of trustworthiness. He keeps them dependent on him in a very unhealthy way. Enthusiasm is discouraged. Their spirit is dulled.

Rather than creating a family atmosphere in the parish, paternalism creates a spirit that makes the family experience impossible. Conformity is substituted for unity. Even though the externals of faith may be uniformly expressed, the people do not experience a sense of communion with one another around their priest. He may be respected as a good provider and an effective administrator, but he will not be loved as a father by anyone. Rather than creating joyful memories with his people, he creates indifference or hurt. There is no place for paternalism in the church. It is a sin against celibacy because it is a sin against the very nature of the church as a community of love.

There is a place, however, for paternity in the church. Unlike paternalism, paternity highlights the priest's role as life-giver and unifier. He is meant to be an enabler of his people, encouraging their gifts and talents for the sake of the Kingdom of God. He is meant to nurture their hopes and dreams so they can become responsible leaders in the church standing alongside himself. A pastor in a parish is meant to be the father of an adult family, sharing the leadership responsibilities in keeping with the specific gifts his people have to bring. For this reason, it is simplistic just to speak of the distinction between priest and laity. There is every bit as much of a distinction between the matrimonied couple and the dedicated single person. All have gifts to offer, and the pastor, as father, is in a unique position to call them forth.

As father of a parish family, a pastor is meant to help create positive memories for his people. He must help them experience what it means to be a part of the family of God. Again, he is in a unique position to help them celebrate times of great joy, like first communions and weddings, but also to help them discover the reality of a loving God in the midst of suffering and loss. If this means laughing and crying with his people, so be it. It will also mean he chooses to live with them in the ordinary events of daily life, showing his loving care by his faithful presence. This is not an extraordinary calling at all. It is lived by any father worthy of the name. It is true that we cannot talk about our fathers without recalling the memories they created as fathers. That is how great priests will be known as well, by the memories they created in their faith-families. By the way, it should be noted here that the point of "father" is not to highlight a priest's maleness. The issue is his relationship to his people.

In so many ways the difference between paternalism and paternity is the desire a priest has to be a father to his people. At least that is where it starts. He must want that kind of relationship more than anything else. When a priest is living his paternity, he will foster unity among his people. He will be able to stand in their midst and lead them in the celebration of their unity in the Eucharist. When the celebration is over, he returns to live with them and to share their lives on a daily basis. When he discovers division among his people, he is the one who calls them to reconciliation, lest the hurt of a few spread like an infection to the whole body. As unifier, his aim is not uniformity of thought or even action. While the one is impossible, the other is often meaninglessly shallow. The unity he is looking for is much deeper than that. He is aiming at unity of persons, a unity of hearts, a sense of belonging that goes beyond differences. His dream is nothing less than Jesus' dream when he prayed, "That all may be one as you, Father, are in me and I in you" (John 17:21).

Be Hopeful Anyway

Even though we all struggle against these very sins that weaken or destroy relationships, we must continue to maintain hope, the God-given desire that they, like any sin, can be overcome. This may mean we will stand alone at times, but we have no other real options. Priests especially cannot afford to let the spirit of pessimism overwhelm them as they try to live a celibate way of life in the church today. They must realize that they are not condemned to a life of privation and loneliness. As celibates, they can choose a way of loving for life. The option is theirs. As men of hope, they can make that choice.

To this end, the following "commandments" may be helpful. They are offered here as a few words of encouragement priests can turn to when their desire to do what is right may be at a low ebb or when the darkness they see in life seems to be overcoming their goodness. When a priest is wondering if it is worth the effort, some of these statements may be just enough to keep him from losing hope. The author of the first eight is unknown. The final two were added to complete the list at ten.

1. People are unreasonable, illogical and self-centered. Love them anyway.
2. If you do good, people will accuse you of selfish, ulterior motives. Do good anyway.
3. If you are successful, you will make false friends and true enemies. Succeed anyway.

4. The good you do today will be forgotten tomorrow. Do good anyway.
5. Honesty and transparency make you vulnerable. Be honest and transparent anyway.
6. What you spend years building may be destroyed overnight. Build anyway.
7. People really need help but may attack you if you really help them. Help people anyway.
8. Give the world the best you have, and you will get kicked in the teeth. Give the world your best anyway.
9. If you choose to live a life of communion with your people, making them the first priority in your life, you will be judged old-fashioned. Live with your people anyway.
10. When you openly proclaim your love for your people, you will be dismissed as hopelessly idealistic. Proclaim your love anyway.

These commandments are not a call to masochism but a call to live the Gospel. When the ultimate command is to "Love one another as I have loved you," someone will always object, someone will always be threatened, someone will always be there to ridicule, someone will always be there to discourage. So if the charism of celibacy is about our loving one another, we can expect it will not be easy to live. Not because it is a sacrifice of our humanity but because it will demand living our humanity to the fullest. With the help of God's grace, we can make that our choice, all pessimism to the contrary notwithstanding. But one thing is for sure: no priest can live it alone.

Appendix:
A Married Clergy

In dealing with the issue of optional celibacy, or optional marriage if you will, a few words of caution are in order. It would be just as irresponsible for a priest to jump into marriage to solve his problems with celibacy as it would be irresponsible for him to think that celibacy, as such, is the source of his problems. Too many truly fine priests have left the priesthood only to experience the pain of short-lived marriages. In fact, the current state of matrimony in the church needs to be examined every bit as much as the current state of celibacy. Both are in need of renewal. Matrimony's is underway. Celibacy's is yet to begin.

Furthermore, there seems to be a natural tension between the priorities a married priest would have to deal with. Who will be his top priority, his people or his wife? Many Protestant ministers are aware of this tension in their lives. Some have no doubt dealt with it effectively, others have not. But this tension would be compounded for a priest because of the nature of priesthood, which calls for a unique kind of intimacy between himself and his people. In addition, Orders and matrimony are sacramental vocations of equal worth. Should this equality be ignored, one or the other could easily be reduced to the status of a second-class sacrament.

It would be a sad mistake to view matrimony as simply a

backdrop out of which a man lived his priestly vocation. It would be a great injustice not only to his marriage but especially to his wife. She would be expected to sacrifice because the faithful needed a priest, even though she needed a husband. The sad consequences of this sort of dynamic are well documented in those marriages where wives regard their husbands' jobs as the greatest competition they have for his affection. They often feel left out. But in the situation when the priest's "job" is his sacred duty, the problem is magnified just that much more.

Similarly, should matrimony become the prime focus of a priest's life, his people would have to sacrifice for the sake of his wife. It is not hard to imagine the faithful becoming critical of their priest's "other spouse." It would bring its own set of problems. Every effort should be made to avoid allowing either of these situations to surface in the church. Again, it must be remembered that the needs of the priest, not to mention his wife's, are only one part of the equation to be considered. The welfare of the faithful and the proclamation of the Gospel to the world must also be taken into account.

If there is a way out of this apparent dilemma, what is it? It seems the option of a married clergy has the best chance of succeeding when both parties accept, in theory and in practice, the fact that matrimony shares equal status with priesthood as a vocation in, of, and for the church. If a married priest is to live his priesthood in a healthy way, his marriage must be equally healthy. Both have important graces to bring to the church. Neither should be compromised for the sake of the other. This means the priest would need a strong spouse, a person of faith, who understands his dreams for the church and is willing to strive with him to model those dreams in the context of their own relationship. She would not be taking a back seat to the faithful nor be regarded as a social appendage to her husband's priestly image.

The faithful, on the other hand, would not view her as a "competitor" for their priest's time. They would see her as sharing the sacrament of matrimony for their sakes with her priest-husband. Rather than take their priest away, she would be helping him to be his best self as priest for them. In other words, this means both spouses are equally committed to their sacramental marriage, seeing it not as a backdrop out of which the vocation of priesthood is lived but as a source of strength and unity that the priest would bring to his people. At the same time, however, a married priest would be expected to bring his wife a vision of church from his relationship with his people that would enrich their relationship as a sacramental couple of the church and for the church.

The primary intimacy for a married priest, however, would be with his wife, not with his people. This is what will truly distinguish his priesthood from that of the celibate priest. A celibate's primary intimacy is with his people, often through those who are closest to him who in a sense represent all his people. Unlike the case of the married priest with his wife, this intimate relationship is neither permanent nor exclusive. It would need adaptation and change during the priest's life. The married priest would serve his people through his wife, as it were. His priestly ministry, not to mention his priestly presence, would be "tinted" or "shaped" by his intimate unity with his wife. While he would still be called to a special relationship with the faithful, a fundamental condition of sacramental priesthood, it would not be his primary intimate relationship.

This is demonstrated, at least in part, by many married deacons in the church today. Most people understand that their primary relationship is still with their wives, not with the faithful, although the sacrament of orders does alter their relationship with them. If there is a cause of concern, it is that many married deacons seem to leave their wives totally out of their deaconal lives. The fact that they are married is often irrelevant to the fact that they are permanent deacons. While some may see this as perfectly acceptable, we see it as a genuine concern. To the extent they do not bring their intimate relationship with their wives to bear on their ministries, their role as married deacons is impoverished. To that extent so also is their marriage. Unfortunately for many wives, the deaconate has become just another reason why their husbands must be away from home.

For a married clergy, it would be wrong to obscure the significance of either orders or matrimony as sacraments for the church. Both deserve to be lived to the full. A married priest could bring something to the faithful that a celibate could not, while the unique gifts of the celibate priest could still be recognized and even treasured by the faithful. One thing, however, should be becoming clear. A celibate priest truly centers his life of faith on his people. They are his life. As his relationship with his people goes, so goes his life. He has no one else to turn to. He has thrown in his lot with them every bit as much as a married priest would with his wife, for better or for worse. It is the charism of celibacy, a gift from God for the sake of the church, that helps, even enables, a man to do this with the confidence that his life will be full.

Rather than compete with or be mutually exclusive of each other, matrimony and orders are actually mutually complementary and can jointly serve the church. A married clergy is possible in the church. But this does not lessen the legitimate place a celibate clergy has in the church. If anything, it highlights it. But before this can happen in reality, there must be an attitudinal shift, on the part of priests especially, about the significance of both matrimony and celibacy in the church. To repeat, the renewal of matrimony and celibacy cannot be taken lightly. There is just too much at stake, not just for the parties involved but also for the unity of the church and its mission to the world. Making that attitudinal shift is really the first option to consider. How we respond to that will determine the fate of optional marriage for the clergy . . . and a whole lot more.

Notes

Chapter 2. Matrimony and Celibacy: Adversaries or Allies?

1. See *Encyclopedia of Theology: The Concise Sacramentum Mundi*, ed. Karl Rahner (New York: Crossroad, 1975), s.v. "Celibacy," by Leonhard M. Weber, p. 179.
2. See Richard P. McBrien, *Catholicism*, Study Edition (Minneapolis: Winston Press), p. 179.
3. See David M. Thomas, *Christian Marriage* (Wilmington, DE: Michael Glazier, 1983), 92.
4. John T. Finnigan, "Marriage/Pastoral Care," *Origins* 5/10 (28 August 1975) 152.

Chapter 4. Masculine, Feminine, or Neuter

1. See John A. Sanford, *The Invisible Partners* (Ramsey, NJ: Paulist Press, 1980), pp. 4–5.
2. Ibid., p. 5.
3. Ibid., p. 7.
4. Richard Rohr, O.F.M., "Nurturing Male Consciousness in Spirituality," talk delivered at the Religious Education Congress for the Archdiocese of Los Angeles at Anaheim, California, 24 March 1984.
5. Archbishop Raymond G. Hunthausen, *Pastoral Letter on the Sacrament of Matrimony* (Elizabeth, NJ: Pastoral and Matrimonial Center, 1982), nos. 68 and 71.

Chapter 6. Fellowship or Communion

1. Cardinal Joseph Bernardin, "Toward a Spirituality of Marital Intimacy," *Origins* 10/18 (16 October 1980) 286.
2. Don Conroy, "Ministry and the Real Priorities of Families," *Origins* 13/5 (16 June 1983) 90.
3. Teresita Scully, "Discernment of Friendships," Human Development 6 (Spring 1985), p. 12.
4. Ibid., p. 6.
5. George A. Aschenbrenner, "Celibacy in Community and Ministry," Human Development 6 (Spring 1985) 27.
6. John Powell, *Why Am I Afraid to Tell You Who I Am?* (Allen, TX: Argus Communications, 1969) and *Why Am I Afraid to Say I Love You?* (Allen, TX: Argus Communications, 1967). The quote is from *Why Am I Afraid to Tell You Who I Am?*, p. 12.